THE
COURAGE
TO BE RICH

Also by Mark O. Haroldsen

Goals, Guts, and Greatness
How to Master Your Financial Destiny
How to Wake Up the Financial Genius Inside You

THE
COURAGE
TO BE RICH

Mark O. Haroldsen

G. P. PUTNAM'S SONS
NEW YORK

The author gratefully acknowledges permission from The
Indianapolis News to reprint material from "Housing Lights
His Fire," by Robert Corya. Copyright © 1982 by The
Indianapolis News.

Designed by Richard Oriolo

Library of Congress Cataloging in Publication Data

Haroldsen, Mark O.
The courage to be rich.

Bibliography: p.
1. Finance, Personal. 2. Investments. 3. Success.
I. Title.
HG179.H317   1983   332.024'01   83-13692
ISBN 0-399-12860-3

Printed in the United States of America

ACKNOWLEDGMENTS

Heaps of thanks need to be given to the many people who played a part in this book's becoming reality, from the two Connies—my agent, Connie Clausen, and Connie Smith, a friend and realtor in Salt Lake City, who encouraged me, then pushed and pleaded and praised me to the completion point of the project—to my oldest son, Mark, who asked me each day if the book was done.

Special thanks also to Dick Lee for his expert help on the tax chapter and to Ellen Hurst for her coordinating efforts and hours of typing. Thanks to Shirlyn Watson, Carolyn Tice, Mary Passey, and Cori Gibson for proofreading and typing. And last but far from least, thanks to the two Dianes, Dianne Higginson and Diane Reverand, who labored so long to edit, rearrange, and make the manuscript more readable, the subheadings more clever.

To my father, Edwin Oliver Haroldsen, for his example of hard work.

To my mother, Kathryn Baird Haroldsen, for her example of love and support, and belief in me.

To Sterling W. Sill, for his example of inspiration and frankness.

And to my children, Mark Ed, Kristin, David Oliver, Nichol, and Camille, who are destined to carry on wherever I may leave off.

CONTENTS

the Obvious? / Lunch at McDonald's / How to Fill Up a Building Fast / Brave Vision / Some MBAs Won't Dirty Their Hands / Fix a Toilet: Make a Fortune / Lots of Hard Work and Coordination / Swimming Pool, Flowerbeds, or Picket Fence / Income Stream Will Tell You What to Do / $40,000 Profit in Six Months / No Second Chance to Make a First Impression / Project Your Profit Before You Buy / A $200-a-Day Penalty Will Work Miracles / Don't Let the Details Slow You Down

PROLOGUE

I think that if you and I had met when I was twenty-seven years old, you would have thought that I was just like everyone else. And I guess I was—at least on the outside. I had an average life, average home, family, car, job, and income. Even on the inside I think I was pretty much average, except that at age twenty-seven something happened. Maybe what Henry David Thoreau said many years ago got to me. He said, "Oh God, to have reached the point of death, only to find that you have never lived at all." Because suddenly at age twenty-seven I could see that I wasn't heading down the road that I wanted to head. So right then and there I decided to be different. I decided that I was going to be financially free and I set a goal to do just that and do it in just three years.

Well I didn't make it, at least not in three years, but by the end of the fourth year I had accumulated a one-million-dollar net worth, which was exactly my objective. On the average I had earned more than $20,800 a month, but more important, I still had all of it left. With my newfound wealth I decided to retire. But my retirement only lasted for three weeks before I decided that retirement wasn't for me. I was bored to death. The local newspaper wrote an article about my rags-to-riches story, which brought dozens of requests for me to explain exactly how I had done it.

I enjoyed telling my story and answering all the questions people had. At least I did for a while. But soon I tired of saying the same thing over and over, so I decided to write a book and tell my story, giving all the details of how I had amassed a million-dollar net worth in forty-eight months. I titled that book *How to Wake Up the Financial Genius Inside You* (also available under the title *Financial Genius*). I didn't want to be turned down by the New York publishers, so I published the book myself, wrote my own ads and, using a big chunk of the money I had earned, set out to sell the book. And sell it I did. A million and a half copies, as a matter of fact, and I added another two million dollars to my net worth.

Now, I know that money certainly doesn't make the man, but it does take a Man, and specifically a man of courage, to rise above the masses today to make millions. What's amazing to me is the large number of men and women who go to the wrong people for financial advice. How much sense does it make to go to a neighbor who's in the same bad financial shape as you, or even to go to a banker, for financial advice? What does a banker know about money? All he does is keep track of it for other people—he is just a custodian of other people's money.

When seeking financial advice, I have found that when I go to men and women who have actually made money, not ones who just talk about money, I have added hundreds of thousands and even millions to my net worth. That is one reason I decided to write this book. Everything I discuss here I have done myself. So I know what I am talking about.

Many individuals, newspapers, and magazines have called me a "financial genius." If combining some simple techniques with courage constitutes genius, then I guess I have to plead guilty. But if being a financial genius means having a high IQ or being a scholar, then I'm innocent. More than two hundred thousand people have attended my seminars and lectures, some paying as much as two thousand dollars. And thousands more have attained financial freedom and are enjoying the benefits that go along with it.

Introduction

COURAGE SEPARATES FINANCIAL DOERS FROM FINANCIAL DUFFERS

A book that shows you how to make money needs to be just as much a psychology book as a finance book; in fact, maybe even more so, since the biggest single factor that is missing in the lives of people who are broke, go broke, or never accumulate enough to be free financially is that lack of courage. Courage is tied to what a person thinks of himself or herself and to habits of fearlessness that are formed by continual self-encouragement. Any average person can hire the best legal mind, the best accountant or business manager or adviser in the country, but what he or she can't hire is guts, or courage.

I have never seen an ad that says, GUTS FOR SALE: LEASE OR LOAN. Courage is not for sale: only you can provide that all-important element.

Courage is what really separates the men from the boys— the financial doers from the financial duffers. *The Courage to Be Rich* will show you how to build your courage and where to apply it today in our chaotic economy.

It takes courage to be rich—and a lot of it. Why is courage so important? If you want to be rich, you have to swim upstream; you have to buck popular opinion. You might *think* that you have courage, but will you have the courage to stand up when the neighbors think you are nuts, when your mother-in-law thinks you are reckless, when your spouse doubts you, and even when your best friends think you will fail and lose everything you own? It's easy to have guts when you're not tested. And it's easy to talk as though you had a lot of spunk. But action is the proof of your courage.

MARK O. HAROLDSEN'S DEFINITION OF COURAGE

Courage is going against the odds, against popular opinion. It's doing what most people are unwilling to do because of the criticism and flak they know they will receive from family, friends, or even strangers. Courage is living your life for you. It's setting your own rules and policies and taking full responsibility when you fail or stumble. It's resisting other people's attempted manipulations of you. Courageous people do not accept all traditions, conventional wisdom, or pat answers without close scrutiny and severe questioning.

THE KEYS TO SUCCESS

A reporter once asked me to give him a list of what I considered to be the keys to success. Here's the list I gave him:

1. Everyone is going to die someday, so you might as well really go for it. Don't be afraid of making a fool of yourself.
2. Guts are not for sale; only *you* can supply that.
3. Don't be afraid to ask questions even if you think they sound dumb—that's how you learn.
4. Use other people's money: always, always, always ask the seller to carry the financing on whatever asset you're buying.
5. Seek out and find motivated sellers—people who want to sell something so badly they are desperate.
6. Earn big bucks by purchasing the "yuks." Find property that nobody else wants; that's where the money is.
7. Use the tax laws to cut your taxes to zero.
8. Success in anything is a numbers game; do it

enough times and you will become good at it; do it a bunch more times and you will become famous.

In the pages that follow, I will develop these themes and will show you how to use these keys to achieve your financial goals.

THE
COURAGE
TO BE RICH

1

THE WORLD WILL STEP ASIDE FOR THE PERSON WHO KNOWS WHERE HE IS GOING

Tennis champion Tracy Austin has a plaque in her bedroom that states, THE WORLD WILL STEP ASIDE FOR THE PERSON WHO KNOWS WHERE HE IS GOING. Tracy Austin obviously followed this philosophy to get to the top of the tennis world. And she did it while still a teenager.

A clear notion of the riches you intend to achieve through your investments will clear your path of people less confident, less sure, than yourself. People meandering along the financial path from paycheck to paycheck will almost always step aside for the earnest, courageous investor.

TRY THE IGDS PHILOSOPHY

You tell me where you want to go financially and I can tell you how to get there. I can even guarantee that you'll make it. If you begin today to use Tracy Austin's philosophy combined with the IGDS philosophy, your success, financial or otherwise, is virtually guaranteed. What is IGDS? It is accepting the truth that "I'm Going to Die Someday." You see, all of us are going to die someday. That's a fact we cannot change. The older we get the more we seem to accept that fact. So why not really live life now? Why not really go for it? Why not? What have you got to lose? Just imagine what you have to gain as you begin moving toward the fulfillment of your potential: you will begin to really live, not just exist.

From the outset of this book I want you to keep in mind the philosophy of IGDS: I am Going to Die Someday—so I might as well go for it now! Think, "My life is now in each moment. I'll fill my moments with good things."

What matters most is that you and I do something great with our lives. You—and that means everyone—have the power to be great. You are totally unique and you are unique for a reason: to do something that nobody else in the world has done. Money or wealth is only a means to an end. Financial freedom for you will buy you the opportunity to discover and exploit your uniqueness and that of your children, parents, and friends. Here is the icing on top of the cake: if you let the IGDS philosophy dominate your thoughts, you'll have an exhilarating time pursuing your financial goals. You'll laugh as you go, all the way to the bank.

FOOLISH FEARS TENSE YOU UP

People fear failure, which makes them timid and self-conscious. They are terrified of making fools of themselves. And that's where the philosophy of IGDS can help: it really doesn't matter if you make a fool of yourself for a moment or even a whole day. We all do foolish things, but that doesn't make us permanent fools. We just did something dumb and we probably learned from it. Think about that right now. I mean, really *think*.

So what if you do something dumb? The fact is that the more you pursue life with great vigor, without fearing failure, the more relaxed you will become and the fewer failures you will have.

HOW A THIRTY-FOUR-YEAR-OLD GETS A QUICK $6000

Take the thirty-four-year-old man who desperately needs some quick cash. He reluctantly calls the local bank for a $6000 signature loan. He's never met the banker and is not exactly sure how to ask for a loan or what interest rates he will be charged—because he has never done this bold a thing before. But with the IGDS philosophy, he blunders ahead. The phone rings. The banker answers and Mr. Thirty-four-year-old asks for a $6000 signature loan at 1% over prime rate. The banker laughs and asks if he is serious, telling him they don't make signature loans in this market and certainly not at that rate. A major failure, right? Maybe it is a failure, but it is not major. A serious setback? Not really. It just doesn't matter. It is merely a temporary setback if Mr. Thirty-four-year-old doesn't give up. Sure he got turned down, but it just doesn't matter.

In fact, now is the time to get the banker to help. Though Mr. Thirty-four-year-old was turned down, how about referrals? "Mr. Banker," he might have asked, "what other banks could I go to? Who specifically should I ask for? Can I use your name as a referral? What interest rate would be reasonable to ask for? Please help me. I need your help. How can I improve my approach?"

The banker is now somewhat on the defensive. He is like an employer who has fired somebody, which is a difficult thing to do. The person being fired, if he or she is smart, will ask for favors at that point because most employers will do just about anything to save their own guilty conscience on the spot.

Some people would look at this call to the banker as a failure because they didn't get the loan on the first bumbling try. Many would feel bad that they were rejected. But so what; who got hurt? It just doesn't matter—at least if the lesson is learned and applied later. Wisdom comes from experience. Skill comes from practice, and it is a skill that you are developing as you pursue the IGDS notion. You become wise *and* courageous.

GO AHEAD, OVERSTUFF YOUR LIFE

Those people who decide to live by the philosophy of IGDS and overstuff their lives with experiences are the ones for whom the world will step aside. Remember: it is not what happens in life, but how you take it. If you expect some setbacks in your life, you'll digest them more easily when they come and they'll hardly slow you down. You might get turned down by ten bankers in a row, or you might get jilted, or you might face a divorce, a bankruptcy, a drawn-out lawsuit, or the untimely death of a loved one. Whatever the external circumstances are, almost everyone has gone through tough times. And I mean tough. If you learn from those experiences and figure out what those so-called disasters are teaching you, life becomes more meaningful. The emotionally strong, the real winners in life, are those who accept the fact that they can't control all external circumstances but know through experience that they can control how they react to circumstances.

"COACH" BELIEVED ME WHEN I SAID I WANTED TO BE RICH

In my late twenties I started to realize that our least-complicated problems are financial, a truth that most people fail to recognize.

I decided to do something about my financial condition, which at the time was a pathetic net worth of approximately $7000. That was the good news. The bad news was that the sum had brackets on both sides of it: ($7000). I didn't know it then, but my decision to make a million dollars by age thirty put me almost halfway there.

YOUR CURRENT DOMINANT THOUGHT

If you know precisely where you want to go financially, and start moving forward (even though you may not know exactly how to get there and will make mistakes along the way), you will come so close to your target or goal that it may scare you. Research has proven over and over that a person moves consistently toward his or her currently dominant thoughts. That's why fat people get fatter and rich people get richer.

MY TWENTY-FOUR-HOUR INNER COACH

When I decided that the nice, round number of one million dollars was what it would take to retire at age thirty, my inner coach said, "Okay, if that is what you want, that is what I'll help you work on." And work on it we did—coach and I.

I didn't realize that he was working on it full time, around the clock. He never stopped. I had some doubts in the back of my mind, but coach didn't have any, not knowing the meaning of the words doubt or escape. He wouldn't let me watch football on TV all weekend. He would make me get out of bed early. He was coaching my thinking about ways to make money almost all the time. He really did believe me. Just by making that decision I had unleashed a twenty-four-hour partner who was relentless in helping me achieve my stated goal.

As I started heading toward that goal, I had many detractors who said that I was crazy and headed for failure. As I became more sure of what I wanted, many of these nay-sayers stood back and watched my smoke. Small newspaper stories began to report my successes. I was labeled a genius or considered just plain lucky. But only I knew about the great power of my inner coach and what "we" could do.

IMAGINATION CAN TRICK YOUR CENTRAL NERVOUS SYSTEM

Inner coaching plus imagining can help you reach your objectives. The central nervous system cannot tell the difference between reality and fantasy. This means you can trick your central nervous system into believing that you are doing things like giving speeches, making presentations for bankers, investors, etc., which in actual fact you are only doing in your mind. Vivid imagining can help you reach your objectives. As far as the control center of your body is aware, you are *actually* doing what you are imagining.

23% IMPROVEMENT WITHOUT EVER TOUCHING A BASKETBALL

The experiment that demonstrated this point involved three groups of students who were each given a basketball and told to throw free-throw shots. Each group shot for the hoop and the percentage of successful throws was tallied. Each group was asked to do something different before repeating this exercise twenty days later: the first group, the control group, was told to go home and forget about it until they were to return. The second group was told to practice throwing the ball every day. The third group was told to spend twenty minutes every day imagining themselves standing at the free-throw line and shooting the basket.

When the control group shot again, their percentage of increase in accuracy was zero, just as would be expected. The second group, which had practiced for twenty minutes each day, improved their accuracy by 24%. The third group, which had visualized themselves shooting successful baskets, improved their accuracy by 23% without ever having touched a ball in the intervening time.

The implication of what this type of visualizing can do for life is nothing short of phenomenal. If you have to choose among several run-down real estate investments for turnaround, visualizing improvement schemes for the various properties can help you save time and money and can help you maximize your investment. If you can visualize yourself asking for a loan or negotiating a complicated deal, you will be gaining experience that will improve your actual performance. Setting your mind on an objective and visualizing it will make your goal easier to achieve.

If you spend enough time internalizing your ideas, they become a part of you and will come to pass. In fact, that is what genius is all about. *Genius is the ability to clearly visualize the objectives.* If we can clearly visualize our cash, income, savings and investment objectives we will be able to actualize our visions.

MAKING A MILLION DOLLARS IS SIMPLE, BUT NOT EASY

Of course, you can imagine all you want, but you must also take action, you must pay the price, you must *do* something to achieve something. I want to emphasize that success in anything takes work and lots of it. Everybody knows that, or at least they should. Although there are always books and programs that promise you an easy road to fame and fortune, we all know that there are toll booths along the way and that driving to a destination is wearying. Making a million dollars is simple, but it's not easy. (See Chapter 4.) The steps to accumulate riches are simple to understand and to follow. Anyone with a ninth-grade mentality can understand these steps, but to go out and act takes effort, discipline, energy, and, let us not forget, courage.

MOST RAGS-TO-RICHES SPEAK WITH AN ACCENT

I can't even begin to count the number of people who have come up to me at seminars and lectures to say "thank you" in broken English. They were thanking me for whatever I had done to help stimulate their minds and subsequently their actions to put the principles and methods of moneymaking into action. Some had added only 500 or 1000 dollars a month to their income. Others had made millions. I started to wonder just what it was that seemed to drive these people who came to this country with an obvious disadvantage.

I DON'T SPEAK VERY GOOD ENGLISH

Senator Jake Garn from Utah told me the following story:

"Mark," he said, "the other day I was picked up by a chauffeur-driven limousine, and as we drove across the city, I started talking with the chauffeur. I must have been complaining to him about unemployment and how tough things were in the economy, because he finally said in his broken English, 'Sir, I probably should not speak but I don't understand Americans. I come to this country three years ago and here many people say impossible to get job. Things are too bad. I wonder about that because I opened up newspapers and see many, many jobs ads. I don't speak very good English then but I go around trying to get hired. I get a job driving limousine. That was three years ago. This year, after working very hard for three years I make $150,000.' "

Well, at this point, the senator was absolutely flabbergasted. "You mean to tell me that you've been in this country only three years and this year you are going to make $150,000 driving a limousine?" he asked. And the man said, "No, no, you don't understand. I am not a chauffeur now. You see, one of my drivers is sick today. I have seventeen others, but today was a very busy day and I had to drive for the sick man."

YOU CAN'T JUST SIT AND END UP RICH BY NEXT TUESDAY

Here is a case of an immigrant who worked his tail off going to night school to learn English and spending his days as a chauffeur. Three years later he owned the business he worked for and is netting $150,000 for his efforts.

There are countless examples of enterprising people who come to this country with very little and who grab opportunities and run with them. A young refugee by the name of Tai Vu, who was getting his law degree in Vietnam, had his studies cut short by the ravages of war. Now Tai Vu lives in Portland, Oregon, where he is a janitor—a very successful janitor, taking in over $500,000 a year. He owns his own company, which maintains restaurants, taverns, and corporate headquarters in Portland. He has been in this country just seven years and already has a half-million-dollar business with sixty employees. He is only thirty-one.

Many people who speak perfect English and are very well educated cry and complain that there is no work available. I guess they're thinking that someone is going to call them to tell them about a job or about an opportunity for starting their own company or making an investment without any of their own cash and that they'll be rich by a week from Tuesday.

Of course it doesn't happen that way. It's not easy. It takes work, struggle, and effort. Super deals and opportunities usually don't get dumped in your lap without any of your own effort. There has probably never been a person making $100,000 or more per year who hasn't asked for it, gone after it, or done some heavy figuring on ways to get it. It doesn't just fall in your lap. It is not luck. It takes work.

AN OVERALL GAME PLAN

Most people aren't afraid of hard work once they get started. It's just that the average American doesn't have the overall game plan to know where to direct his or her energy and efforts. Most people spend more of their time planning their vacation or even a weekend than they spend planning their financial life. If you can put that same energy into financial planning and combine it with sweat to carry out those plans, you will find yourself well on your way to financial independence.

BEYOND INCOME

Most people, when setting financial goals, make the big mistake of setting only income goals. "I am making $27,000 this year. If I can only stretch myself and end up making $35,000, I would be tickled to death." Once a person has understood that the real money, large amounts of it, comes from sources other than his own labor, he becomes wise and starts setting more than just income goals.

Basically, a person should have three sets of goals—income, savings, and investments, as shown in Graph 1.

In the bar at the far left of Graph 1, you see a *level-of-income goal*. Whatever level of income you choose, a certain percentage should be set aside for cash savings. Whether it is 10% or 15% is up to you. The larger the amount you begin with, the more quickly you will realize your overall financial

Graph 1

Financial Goals
(3 Sets)

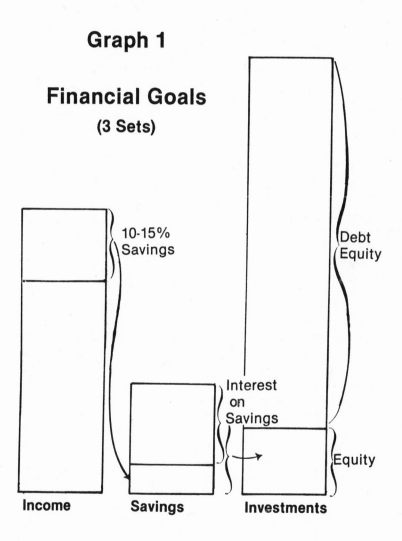

10-15%
Savings

Debt
Equity

Interest
on
Savings

Equity

Income   **Savings**   **Investments**

goals. You will find that it is important to save the maximum amount now.

The bar in the center shows your *savings goals,* and indicates not only the savings from your income, but also the growth of those savings from interest. This can be fairly substantial, especially in times of high inflation when 10%, 12% and even 18% is paid on savings accounts. If you buy the right kind of certificate or instrument, your return on savings can be substantially increased, even above the 18% level. As you will learn later in this book, there are ways to earn even more interest.

The right-hand bar shows your *investment objectives.* Here you see how some cash savings have been funneled off to buy appreciating assets. In addition to the savings that you are using to buy these assets, the bar shows a large amount of debt equity, which is borrowed money used to buy the appreciating assets that eventually will become equity as the debt is paid down. On top of that is the appreciation, shown by the broken line. Inflation is the cause of this appreciation.

Many people set a goal of making a million dollars, not realizing that the wiser goal would be to achieve a specific amount of passive income generated by assets that you own. For example, rather than saying you want to make a million dollars, you would say, "I want to buy appreciating assets that will eventually give me $150,000 a year in income without any substantial effort on my part."

When setting such goals, never forget to set a time limit. Remember, your self-coach is working with you and needs to know what the time frame is—or you just might take your entire life to do it.

With this overall game plan in mind, you should be ready to work on your courage factor.

2

COURAGE IS THE CLOUT OF CHAMPIONS

Courage is being so stubborn that you simply won't accept defeat. It is the stuff that makes champions in sports, war, business, and in life. With it you can do almost anything. Without it even a brilliant man accomplishes little.

TAKE HEART

Our English word "courage" comes from the French word for heart. Great-hearted, or stouthearted, or stronghearted people have courage—a lot of heart. Criticism can't turn the courageous from their path. They have self-reliance and are willing to be responsible for their choices. The courageous have the heart to choose their own course of action. They believe in themselves and are free from the entangling influence of others. They pull their own strings. Those with courage are not afraid to risk.

Courage is the major separator. That's why so many very bright people with good connections and ready sources of cash for investments are upstaged by "C" students or school dropouts who have courage.

Most great courageous acts we read about are very physical, involving war heroes, amazing athletic achievements, or handicaps overcome. I don't want to minimize this kind of bravery, but sometimes some of us ordinary people are so busy looking for a chance to show our courage in some very dramatic and visible way that we fail to see that courage can be demonstrated in our everyday struggles.

To be rich may well take more courage and be more difficult than for a man to jump into a rushing river to save a child. To be rich takes more than a sudden burst of courage that may be just a reaction to the circumstances. To be rich involves sustained risk-taking.

HEAD BATTLES

Most battles are fought in our minds. If you want to achieve more than the average person, the battles are tougher. If you are striving for anything out of the ordinary, the average person will never understand what you are up to. And that will make you question yourself. So your head battle will continue for a while. You will wonder whether you're doing the "right" or "best" thing. You will constantly be asking yourself: Should I invest my savings? What will people say if I fail? Should I pursue this new business full-time? What if I run out of cash and lose everything? What if there is another depression? Am I being fair to my kids? Will my wife (or my husband) leave me if I don't do well? Who am I to think that I can succeed where others have failed? Nobody in my family has ever done anything like this before. What if I get sick? How am I going to live without any salary when the money stops coming in? And on, and on, and on. Courage takes firmness of spirit.

Think about it and you'll see how much courage it takes to fight those mental battles to achieve your immediate or long-range goals to become totally financially free. Obviously it can be done because so many people have done it. And so many people have made it by starting at absolutely rock bottom.

KEYS TO COURAGE—AND TECHNIQUES

Fortunately there are some keys to courage that make it easier to improve that quality in ourselves. Most of the keys to courage are variations on the theme of positive self-expectancy, of believing in one's self, being optimistic; expecting the very best; expecting to win; expecting better jobs, family relationships, health; expecting more money. In short, positive mental attitudes show courage. We get what we expect from life.

Dr. Denis Waitley, the space-age psychologist, has outlined some techniques for improving positive self-expectancies. Let me explain four such techniques:

1. Be a reverse paranoiac: look at problems as opportunities. Greet bad news as good news, then find out what opportunities that news holds.

2. Keep yourself relaxed and friendly in spite of tension and pressure. Calmness and courage are *learned* habits.

3. Speak positively of things—use praise. Avoid griping. Avoid self-pity.

4. Share your excitement over your own dreams. Enthusiasm is infectious. Cheerfulness cheers others and reinforces you.

PEOPLE BUILDERS

Surround yourself with people who demonstrate courage in their lives, people who build other people up and don't tear them down. All of us need people around us who think that we are tremendous, people who will support us, because there is not one of us who goes through life without some downers. No, we don't need to have flatterers around us, or yes-men. What we need is people who genuinely see the best in us and remind us of that best from time to time, especially when we need it.

I have several dear friends who are on my people-builders list. They not only build me up when I need it, they build up many others. That's the kind of list everybody needs. So sit down and write out your own list and then cultivate those relationships. Spend time with these people. It will change your life. It should go without saying that you need to be a people builder also. And if you are, it is easy to get people to be on your list.

CHOOSING THE RIGHT-MIND ROAD

The unique thing about the human mind is its ability to pick and choose what it wants to think about and what it wants to dwell upon. You can choose which mental road you WANT to go down.

Our thoughts are linked together. In fact, that is how our memory works. Consider your favorite record album. You know every song in the order that it appears on that album. You might not be able to tell me right now what the order is, but as one song gets close to its end, your mind will automatically tell you what the next song is going to be. Since the mind has the ability to stay on one road for some time and link thoughts, when you find yourself on the wrong mental road, *stop and get off it*. Get on the mind road that is courage building. That is a mind road that is positive, that will take you places that are good for you.

We do in fact control the mental road that we go down. And I don't care if you have recently gone through a divorce, the death of a loved one, a business failure, a heart attack, a cancer operation, or are $17 million in debt. Or all of the above! Though you may be feeling miserable, you have to realize that you can get off that road. You *can* choose which road your mind will take.

BELIEVE IN YOUR OWN DESTINY

Believe in your own destiny, and your courage factor will soar to great heights. After you set your goals, believe in them so profoundly that timidity won't stand in your way.

If you study great men and women in history, you find that many claimed to have had peak experiences that assured them of their own destinies. After such peak experiences, their belief in themselves—their courage—was strengthened, in spite of persecution from others.

Dr. David Campbell, in his book *Take the Road to Creativity and Get Off Your Dead End,* says that creative people, or the so-called dreamers, seem to have "a sense of destiny and this sense of destiny creates momentum that fuels persistence, overcomes failure, persuades ordinary mortals to do the leader's or creator's will." (He thinks there are a lot more people who are creative than think they are.)

Creative people, the doers in life, tend to have a great sense of their own destiny. The stronger the sense of that destiny, the greater a person's courage. *The key is to start believing in yourself, start spending time thinking of your own life and what it means in the greater scheme of things.* What is your contribution to be? Why are you here? Certainly it's to do more than breathe air and take up space.

THE DREAMER WINS, THE TRADITIONALIST LOSES

I'll never forget the comments made by an attorney when I was recently trying to buy a fairly sizable property. The attorney, who was representing the owner, called after he had received our purchase offer. He called because he couldn't believe what he was seeing. On the purchase offer, I had asked the seller to carry back some of the financing at zero-percent interest on a substantial amount of money. At the time I made the offer, I was doing a bit of dreaming, but I had to. The only way the deal would work was by his carrying back that fourth mortgage at zero-interest rate or by substantially dropping the price, which he had refused to do. The attorney was astonished by the audacity of such a ridiculous offer.

What was his response? His main concern was that he had never seen such an offer; he was flabbergasted by it. When I assured him that I make offers and deals like this all the time (a slight exaggeration), his comment (which shocked me out of my shoes) was, "Well, in that case then I'll talk to my client about it." You see, he was more concerned about whether this kind of thing was done, whether it was traditional or not, rather than how the numbers would affect him and his client. He was a traditionalist through and through. In this case I was a dreamer because I didn't think that I could get the property. I was doing a lot of wild "what-if" thinking.

Some time ago I went to a seminar in the Midwest conducted by Joe Sugarman, the highest-paid marketing and advertising writer in the United States. In the seminar Joe described the type of people who are the big successes in life.

There are basically three kinds of people: (1) the traditionalist, who is more concerned about how things have been done in the past and holding to those traditions, (2) the catalyst, the person who is always trying to get people together, an arranger of people and meetings, and (3) the dreamer or creative person, who is always trying to find a better way, who is always challenging tradition and wondering why things can't be done a different way. He went on to say that none of us are all of one type. There is mixture in most of us. As I studied myself and my associates, what he said seemed to make a lot of sense. Creative dreamers are the big successes in life when they act on their dreams and fulfill them.

MONEY AND YOUR GUILT

I find one of the biggest single mental struggles that people have when it comes to setting financial goals and going after them is their own guilt feelings. Somehow they think or have been taught that something is wrong with making money. If you have been taught or believe directly or indirectly that money is evil, then you need to evaluate why you believe that. Who told you that? What authority did they have? Who has set themselves up as the interpreter of what you should do? This kind of reasoning and thinking takes a lot of courage because it goes against the crowd. If you start practicing, you will find that there is great strength in this attitude. You will become a much more confident individual, able to take total responsibility for all your actions and their consequences.

"YEAH, BUT THEY CHEATED"

Is there something wrong with getting rich quick? Why is it that most people seem to think that to get rich quick is bad, especially in light of the fact that most people would love to get rich quick? "You probably have to be dishonest or a crook to get rich quick" seems to be the opinion of many. But is that a fact? Do you need to be dishonest to accumulate a large estate in a short time? The answer is no. The truth is that most people when confronted by someone who has made a fortune in a short period of time think they need to justify why they haven't also. It's so simple to sit back and dismiss other people's achievements and thereby excuse yourself by saying, "Yeah, but they cheated or walked all over people to make the money they made. I am not going to do that, because I think it's wrong."

CREATE YOUR OWN WEALTH AND TAKE SOME FLAK

People like this will probably never change their opinions, and as you rapidly increase your net worth, you are bound to take some flak. Some people will never have a high opinion of you. If they did, how would they justify their failure? There are some things that you simply can't do anything about, that you cannot change. One of the big ones is other people's opinions of you. *What other people think of you is their problem.* They believe what they want, whether you like it or not. You can do your best to treat them as you would like to be treated, and to reason with them, but you can't afford to compromise yourself by trying to influence them. Since you're not in charge of their opinions, why be upset by them? Your self-image and self-esteem are far more important than their mistaken views.

The independence that goes along with courage will help you to polish your timing, as you will see in the next chapter.

3

THE CROWD IS ALWAYS A DAY LATE AND A DOLLAR SHORT

TIMING: THE RIGHT MINUTE CAN SAVE AN HOUR

You've probably done it too at a ball game, concert, or any big event. When the event is just about finished, you head for the exit a minute or two before it is officially over. Because of that sixty- or 120-second head start, you ended up home thirty minutes or even an hour earlier than if you had waited a few seconds longer to leave. Those few seconds put you in the parking lot ahead of the crowd, so instead of waiting in snarled traffic, you zipped out without a single stop, onto an uncluttered highway, quickly and safely home.

I have done this a hundred times and saved countless hours, hours that I have used for better things than sitting in parking lots or backed up on city streets or freeways. I have always tried to be a few minutes ahead of the crowd, or, if that is impossible, a long way behind it.

GOLD AND GOLDEN TIMING

Timing can really be everything. It is one of the keys to financial success. If you bought a beachfront property in Honolulu in 1979 and sold it in 1981, you no doubt made a fortune. But if you bought it in 1981 and sold it in 1983, you made little if anything.

In 1980 I flew to Phoenix to get away from the snow and the cold of Utah. While staying at a tennis ranch, I met an interesting, well-educated couple from the East. We all enjoyed the warmth of the Arizona sun and the good tennis, but this couple was particularly overjoyed because of the phenomenal money they had made in the past few weeks from the rapid rise in gold prices. They had bought a lot of gold when it was selling for about $400 an ounce, and now it had shot up over $700.

Since they knew that I had written some financial books and lectured on the subjects of making money and investments, they wanted to know what I thought about the current price of gold. I told them that I certainly was not an expert on gold and really didn't know much about it, but I did know a little bit about people, emotions, and timing. So when they pressed further for my opinion about where gold would go from the $700 mark, I told them that it seemed to me that the market was at or very near the top.

How did I know this? Certainly some of it was from instinct, but that instinct was educated by observing how the gold market had gone crazy. It seemed that everybody was talking about gold—everybody was either buying or knew somebody who was buying. So-called experts were predicting that the price would shoot to $1500. Some of them were saying even to $2000 an ounce.

"The market's too wild for me," I said, "and it seems that something has gotta give." We talked on and on about the subject, and I could plainly see that they weren't about to sell their gold. Well, it is always nice to be right. But I really didn't expect to be so right so quickly. Within weeks of returning home from Phoenix, I watched the price of gold plummet.

This unfortunate lack of timing happens every day in every city in the country, with most types of investments. (They say that only the liar buys at the bottom and sells at the top.) Sure, the couple from the East probably continued to hold their gold until it was back up above their cost. Someday, possibly, they will sell it. Timing really is critical, but it is more critical with certain types of investments than with others. Gold and silver, stocks and commodities, are particularly time-sensitive. For this reason (and many others that will be discussed in later chapters) the average person has a much greater chance of success in markets that do not have such wide swings in such short time periods.

NO RAPID FLUTTER IN PROPERTY VALUES

If, for example, you had bought Warner Communication stocks on the wrong day in December 1982, you would have paid about $63 a share for it. A few days later you would have found that your investment was worth only $40, and by the end of the month you would have lost more than half, because the stock had sunk to $27. On the other hand, in all my years of buying income-producing property, I have never seen any property lose half its value in a few days or even a few months. That is not to say that there are not better times to buy property than others. But when buying the right type of assets, which don't fluctuate so rapidly, you have the advantage of having more time to make decisions. Plus—this is a big plus—with income-producing properties or your own small business you can counteract bad times by better management. Timing is important; but even if you miss the timing when buying the right appreciating assets you can consistently build your net worth without major setbacks.

OTHER PEOPLE WILL WANT TO DREAM YOUR DREAMS

There will always be people who will try to control your mind and beliefs if you let them. They will try to have your own visions. In order to recognize the best timing, you need to be your own person, to do your own thinking and be totally responsible for yourself. You just flat-out can't do that if you are always looking to other people for the answers. You have got to use your own mind to do some thinking. You have got to use your own God-given talents, including instinct and gut feel. They are more accurate and important than you have ever given them credit for.

I am amazed at the number of people who throw themselves into, or even devote their whole lives to, someone else's cause. When you watch them, it seems that they have more allegiance to the various causes than to themselves. You get the impression that the cause or organization is greater than the individuals that make it up. But stop and think about that. Why can't an individual have his or her own cause? And is it not true that individuals are each greater than the organization that they themselves create?

I see so many men and women who watch organizations have fund-raisers, buy properties, form new and exciting enterprises, and create financial empires. People don't seem to understand that they can do the same thing themselves. They hide behind the organization. It certainly doesn't take courage to do that. Rewards are equal to the amount of courage expended. Big courage brings big rewards, both personal and financial.

If you are aware that you are shifting responsibility to an organization, stop it. Unless you do, you won't ever become your own person and reap the financial rewards that are available to men and women who rely on themselves. Many people get so caught up in organizational rules and regulations that they lose sight of their overall goals and their standards. Don't let that happen to you as an individual.

KNOW YOURSELF AND YOU CAN BE YOUR OWN FINANCIAL COACH

Adam Smith said, "The first thing you have to know is yourself. A man who knows himself can step outside himself and watch his own reactions like an observer." This is particularly true in financial matters. You need to be aware of what is going on with yourself before you can recognize what is happening in the financial marketplace.

Ralph Waldo Emerson said, "Whosoever would be a man, must be a nonconformist. . . . Nothing is at last sacred but the integrity of your own mind." Being a nonconformist, you must question everything, especially conventional wisdom. What the masses are thinking at any particular time is usually wrong.

TRADING ON TRENDS

You must look for the trend in what people want. In order to make money, you must supply their wants before the trend is known—when everyone else is supplying that same want.

The nonconformist—the person who can think for himself—always looks for changes in trends. This is done by observation and an awareness of what is going on. I'll never forget a conversation I had with a cabdriver on Maui. Our conversation quickly turned to real estate because it was such a hot item in the Islands. Prices were soaring at a rate that was hard to keep up with. The entire market bothered me. I was shocked when the cabdriver told me he had been offered over $250,000 for a small two-bedroom condo he had owned only eighteen months. He said he would make over $100,000 if he chose to sell, but thought he would hang on a little longer because he was sure that it would go up even more. That was my key to understanding that the market was about to change direction. My reasoning was this: if a man who obviously had not spent much time studying the market could casually make that much money with very little effort, it was just about time for a bust. If that condo had rented for an amount more than, or even equal to, the mortgage payment, I would not have reacted so strongly. But at the time it was selling for two-and-a-half times what it should have been relative to the income that it could generate. Well, to my surprise the crazy market continued for another six months. But prices in fact did drop and they dropped quickly. Many people lost hundreds of thousands of dollars and many others held on by continuing to make payments.

Years ago I discovered The Art of Contrary Thinking, which has been a major guide in my financial life ever since. The philosophy is very simple: *see what the majority of people are thinking, then consider the opposite side as where the truth might be found.* That system is not foolproof, but it certainly has served me well in financial matters.

The stock market is a good example of the majority being wrong most of the time. You see, most people would rather not put themselves into a high-risk position. We all try to avoid situations that make us uncomfortable physically, socially, or financially. So the crowd always tends to wait until it is safe—until it *thinks* it is safe—based on popular opinion, what the majority is doing, or what the majority's confidence factor is at the moment. They do this before putting their hard-earned money into stocks and bonds or in any business investment or venture.

But waiting that long will almost always be too late. The crowd is always late enough to have missed out on making hundreds of thousands, or even a million dollars. What's more, the crowd will always be late and short.

GREATER-FOOL MARKETS

From time to time people will argue with me about the contrary-thinking philosophy by showing me how they have made or are making hundreds of thousands of dollars by participating in the same market as the masses. I call those markets "greater-fool markets." That is, you buy something high and you sell it higher. You sell it at a higher price to a greater fool than yourself. I don't have any qualms about people who play that game, although I usually don't play it myself. The advice I would give if you insist on playing the greater-fool game is to make sure that you are nimble and quick. When things turn sour, you could get stuck with an asset that you can't sell.

WATCH THE MAGAZINE COVERS: THEY BLOW IT EVERY TIME

The national general news magazines (not the specialty financial magazines) are a good barometer of crowd thought. The general news media are a natural barometer because it is the job of the media to report what people are doing and talking about, what the trends are. Most people buy the talk. The national magazines seem to be consistently wrong, so consistently, in fact, that they can be used as an indicator of either a present change in direction or of one to come. I have seen it happen many times. On September 9, 1974, the comment "The Big Bad Bear Crashing Its Way Down a One-Way Street Through the Stock Market" made the cover of *Newsweek* only a few days before the market bottomed.

WHEN EVERYONE OWNS CRADLES, CRADLES WILL FALL

What signals a dramatic change or reversal in a trend? When just about everybody already owns stocks, condos in Hawaii, or gold and silver, you simply run out of buyers. Naturally, buyers are needed to push the price higher or even to keep it where it is. When you run out of buyers, prices obviously fall. That's why I say we need to recognize trends in their beginning stages, before *Time* Magazine puts them on the front cover. It takes contrary thinking and observing to do this, because when a market is at the top, it's hot and everyone is positive about it. They reason, "How could it go down now when everyone is positive?'' Remember the answer—''If everyone owns, there are no buyers left.'' Many of these buyers, I might add, bought in at the tail end of the trend because of the herd mentality. They were afraid of missing out.

PROFITS FROM THE PROPHETS OF DOOM

Prophets of doom and gloom always seem to yell the loudest just before the beginning of prosperity. They proliferate just when things are at their worst. Why? It's simple. They are capitalizing on crowd behavior.

These pessimists don't get much of a hearing when things are going well. If you are making money day after day on your investments, you don't want to listen to their sorry predictions. But when times are bad, it is easier to scare people, so they give the public what it wants. They realize, as Bernard Baruch said, that ''all economic movements by their nature are motivated by crowd psychology.'' Baruch quotes Schiller's dictum: ''Anyone taken as an individual is tolerably sensible and reasonable—as a member of a crowd, he at once becomes a blockhead.''

The doomsayers recognize this crowd psychology, this collective folly, and cash in on it. By observing them, you can more easily predict turnarounds in the marketplace.

EGO CAUTIONS TOO LITTLE ACTION

So learn to watch the trends and to recognize when people become overly pessimistic or way too optimistic. Sure, there will be crosswinds, not a consistent front blowing at you. But you have to contrary-listen to what the majority of people are saying. That's why you look at national general interest magazines.

After you recognize these trends, what should you do about them? What should you buy or sell, and exactly when? First of all, you can't be exact. Don't expect it. You will be disappointed. People and their moods are not an exact science. People who worry too much and take too much pride in being exactly right usually lose money. With that ego-bound attitude comes too much caution and too little action. If your ego gets in the way that much, you are not going to do very well. Here's where you need to step back from yourself, observe yourself, and be your own counselor or coach. Your coach will tell you if you want to be "rich and famous." Paradoxically, you'll have to avoid letting your ego get in the way.

IF THE CROWD IS ALWAYS WRONG—WHEN SHOULD I START?

Any time is a good time to start compared with never starting at all. The emphasis again should be placed on the particular deal. What is it you are starting with? You might sense that the downtrend is just under way; nonetheless a particular deal could be so attractive because of the price and terms that you might still want to go ahead and buy. After all, no one, including you, knows how long the downtrend will last. And if the particular deal is good enough, and you have looked at your risks and have cut them as much as possible, what do you have to lose?

WHEN DOES SMART MONEY START?

Baron Rothschild, who for many years ran the European Rothschild bank said, "Buy when there is blood in the streets." My mentor, Larry Rosenberg, says Rothschild's words still apply today. But Larry goes one step further. He thinks you can always find "blood in the streets" somewhere in the United States in a market, a particular business, or a certain type of venture. He says that he is still as convinced today—in fact more so than twenty years ago—that the key is to "buy the stuff that no one else wants." Larry knows what he is talking about. With his brother, Lew Rosenberg, he controls almost $50 million worth of appreciating assets throughout the United States. They built their empire from an absolute standing start. They had nothing. In fact, if you press them really hard, you will find that they borrowed the first $5000 for their beginning investment and the entire balance of that initial purchase was done through other people's money.

PRECISION TIMING IS NOT NECESSARY WITH ALL INVESTMENTS

You need to get started and you need to get started now. But you have to buy the right kind of appreciating assets.

It may seem that I am saying two contradictory things: (1) that timing is important, so buy only at the right time, and (2) start immediately no matter what is happening now. Actually, both are important. Take a micro-look at your finances. Pay attention just to the deal you are working on. If you find it makes sense, if you can tell that it is a bargain based on the income flow from that particular investment, then you should do something about it now, regardless of the macro-economic outlook. In other words, *the economy can be in a recession, with things getting worse day by day, and you can still do very well financially on a specific deal for a business or income property.*

BOTTOM IS BEST

How can all of this help you, the reader? Obviously the best time to buy an asset, whether it is a business or a property or whatever, is at the bottom of the cycle during the lowest part of a recession. The problem is, no one really knows for sure where the bottom lies. Only in hindsight do we know that the month when things were so bad was in fact the bottom. The financial wizards, the economists, and the PhDs don't know. When the market is at its lowest point, half of them will tell you one thing and half of them will say the exact opposite. So what is a poor guy to do to try to figure it all out?

When I first began buying, I had no idea what part of the business cycle we were in. All I knew was that I needed to get started. Sure, it would have been great if it had been at the very bottom of the cycle. It would have been easier to make money. I didn't even bother to try to figure out what part of the cycle we were in.

DESPERATION IS SURE

Looking back now, I know that if I had waited for the bottom of the cycle there would probably have been so much pessimism in the thinking of the masses and the press that I would have been talked out of beginning. When things are at the bottom, pessimism is so bad that everybody is totally convinced they are going to get worse. It takes a good deal of courage to buck that emotional or mental trend. By then, most have sold, gone bankrupt, or been foreclosed. Everyone has taken all the

color of his or her eyes. When the witness is asked to take time and to think carefully, tracing the steps back in his mind, he can often probe his mind to retrieve the stored data.

Our minds are like computers. Many times we can search and find things that we didn't even know were there. During brain operations, a probe can touch a certain part of the brain of a patient under a local anesthetic, which will stimulate the recollection of details and events long since past. Likewise, under pressing questioning, the eyewitness will usually end up saying, "Yes, now I remember he had on a green shirt, his eyes were blue, and he had a scar over his right eye," etc.

When we "trust our gut," or use instinct, assuming we have trained ourselves to go against the crowd, our subconscious mind seems to take into account all those little factors that we might have missed. It spits out the "feeling" to buy or sell, get more liquidity, or take whatever action seems to be appropriate. How many times have we said or heard said, "I just knew I was doing the wrong thing. . . . I could *feel* it."

FINANCIAL INSTINCTS

We need to trust our gut more in our financial dealings. Consider your ability to pick up on the moods and feelings of others. Consider all the newscasts you have watched and magazines and newspapers you have read. Your internal computer is working twenty-four hours a day, and if you feed in the right philosophy, or your overall objectives, your instinct won't let you down. True, your internal computer won't necessarily give you the precise timing, but you really don't need that. That is, you don't need it if you buy the right kind of assets, the kind of assets that have appreciated over the years and will make you rich. But your instinct will tell you in many cases whether to buy a particular deal. Or whether the people you're dealing with are telling you everything. Instinct can increase income—if you listen to it then act without fear. Go ahead, trust your gut—it's getting more input from your brain than you know!

HOW TO KNOW WHAT TO BUY

Men and women of courage in the past and in the present have bought appreciating assets, but they knew that to make millions they had to buy unique ones and buy them in unique ways. They bought those appreciating assets that nobody else seemed to want at that particular moment. Then they took those assets and transformed them so they were desirable, so everybody wanted them. In a way, they forced the appreciation by two- or threefold (and more). That takes some thinking. And it takes what the world calls creativity. If you don't think that you are creative, you probably are wrong. Creativity is merely the process of relating two known things that are normally unrelated. (See Chapter 7 on "How Yuks Can Create Big Bucks.")

The key to wealth is ownership. You must own something. Ideally, it must be something that is exclusive or unique; something that cannot easily be duplicated by others. Look at the fortunes of men from past days and see how they made their money. They owned things, unique things. For example:

Patents. The cornerstone to Howard Hughes' fortune was a patent his father owned on a special drill bit that was designed to cut through rock and earth in such a way that was virtually unstoppable. None of the competition had such a drill. The Hughes family was very wise. They never sold the drill to anyone. They kept the drill and the patent, and then leased it to others, thereby having a monopoly for years on that particular drill design. What did they own? They owned a patent that gave them an exclusive legal right to their invention.

Xerox Corporation had a huge head start on all the other copying businesses because they were the first to invent the dry copier. By protecting it with patents, they monopolized the market for years, giving them their head start.

Copyrights. The copyright gives you the right to eliminate competition for a number of years. No one else can sell what you have a copyright on without your permission. And anyone who wants to copyright something can do it very easily. Even if you sit down and write a simple one-page letter, and then put a "c" with a circle around it, the date, and your name, you have just copyrighted that letter. It is exclusively yours and that right is protected by law. But of course no one is going to pay you for that one letter unless it is so unique that other people want it. But if you write a book or a series of papers that have real value, value enough to make other people want them, then you have a little monopoly. Knowing this, it is important to take the time and pains to make whatever you want to copyright very,

very good, something that fulfills a need, so that other people will want it and pay for it. Then, by copyrighting it, it is exclusively yours.

Real Property. Real property can be another mini-monopoly. You and you alone own it, albeit with encumbrances against it in the form of loans. But the simple fact is that you have the exclusive right to the property. You can do to that property exactly what you want. You can fix it up, you can change its use, you can make it larger or smaller. It's yours. You can rent it or lease it for a long or a short time. It tends to have an ever-increasing value because the space that it occupies and the dirt underneath it are in limited supply. As Will Rogers said many years ago, "You ought to buy land because they ain't making it anymore."

Property is one of the easiest mini-monopolies to control, especially if it is the right kind of income-producing property. That income can pay off the loans against the property, which is something that most investments can't claim to do. Many people buy property just to profit from the increase in value owing to the limited supply and inflation. But even without any increase in value, income property can be your cornerstone to wealth simply because the tenants pay off the loan. So eventually you end up with assets worth thousands or more, from which you can sell or collect income. When the loan is finally paid off, income increases. Granted, this is a very slow way to gain wealth, but this assumes zero inflation and no effort to improve the property.

The big benefit of real property is that it has intrinsic value. It fulfills the great need of housing, of sheltering human beings, which is always in great demand. Sure, there are times when it is in greater demand than others. And there are times when the demand is weak. But for the small investor, it is probably the safest way to build his or her fortune today, with or without inflation.

YOUR OWN BUSINESS—A TERRIFIC ASSET

Unfortunately, there are many people in the world who will try to talk you out of owning your own business. They tell horror stories about the large number of businesses that go bankrupt within their first seven years. No question about it, there are a number that don't make it. There are also thousands that do make it and make it big. There are many that net $10,000 plus a month for the owner, over his or her salary.

The most commonly accepted reason for new-business failures is undercapitalization. But that is not really the root of the problem. They fail because the person starting the business didn't do all he or she should have done to make the business survive. A smart owner can get capitalization.

The more unique the business you start in terms of its product or service, its systems, its management, and its motivated employees, the more likely that it will succeed. There are many successes that you never hear about—after all, would you be anxious to tell the whole world about your little gold mine or money tree if you knew it was easily susceptible to competition?

I have started a number of businesses, product lines, and corporations, and I find that there are great opportunities out there and that it really isn't that tough to succeed. However, it *is* tough if you follow much of the conventional wisdom surrounding how to start and run a small business.

SKITTLE THE SKEPTICS

The first problem that you are up against when starting your own business is the skeptics who try to talk you out of doing what you want to do. There are bunches of them out there. They want to talk you out of some great ideas, possibly because they have tried themselves and have failed. If you go out and succeed where they failed, that's going to make them look pretty bad, and they don't want to look bad.

Here again, courage is a key, because without courage, you are going to be easily talked out of your ideas. If Thomas Edison hadn't had courage, he would have stopped shortly after he began. The president of prestigious Stevens Institute of Technology discouraged the idea of the electric light bulb by saying, "Everybody acquainted with the subject recognizes it as a complete failure." How do you suppose Edison felt—especially on days when he was down after failing for the thirtieth or fiftieth time?

I'm sure most people would have given up, and done so with ample justification. But, obviously, Edison didn't give up. He believed in himself and had the courage to pursue his goal.

4

THE FALLACY OF WORKING FOR A LIVING

WEALTH FORMULA

Millionaires are not ten, fifty, or a hundred times smarter than you, nor do they work that much harder or longer than you. There are not enough hours in the day for a millionaire to work ten times longer than you. There are only 168 hours in a week, 8736 hours in a year, and no one gets any more. If you have a normal IQ, it would be impossible for someone to be 10 or 100 times smarter than you. The numbers don't go that high.

Why then can people make a million dollars in a relatively short period of time? They just know the wealth formula.

WAGE SLAVES

In *The Lazy Man's Way to Riches,* Joe Karbo observes, "Most people are so busy earning a living, they never make any money." Most people are wage slaves, slaves to their salaries, which just barely cover their living expenses. (And sometimes they don't even do that.) So the wage slave struggles his or her entire life just to break even, and ends up at age sixty-five or seventy with a small pension, a gold watch, and not much to look forward to. By then, everything has grown so expensive that the pension doesn't stretch very far.

FEARFUL SECURITY

Many people don't strike out on their own or undertake what they really want to do in life because of fear. They think they have security because of a salaried or hourly wage job. Consider for a minute how secure that position really is. Consider yourself and your own job. If you were to become ill and were in bed for the next seven or eight months, would you still have a paycheck? Are you really that secure? And most people don't have even that much security. If they make any major mistakes on their job, or the economy delivers a blow to their employer, two weeks' notice is about all the "security" they have.

THE FALLACY OF WORKING FOR A LIVING

Not long ago, I was in a publisher's office in New York City. I noticed on the editor's wall an ad with the headline, THE FALLACY OF WORKING FOR A LIVING. It grabbed my attention and I thought about it for some time after. The fallacy consists in believing that if you work you will have a good living. It is one of the great myths perpetuated in our society that working long, hard hours will make you wealthy. Working long, hard hours for someone else can leave you very disillusioned when you end up poor.

A friend of mine living in Southern California learned the hard way. Nevertheless, he was glad for the lesson. He was a wage slave when he suddenly became sick and found himself in a hospital bed day after day, week after week, month after month. He realized as he lay on his back that his paycheck was soon coming to an end. The few assets he had accumulated would be consumed very quickly. He had always thought that he was secure in his job, since he was hardworking, always first on the job and the last to leave. But now this. He realized that he had been a wage slave all through the years. He didn't own anything. He didn't have appreciable assets built up to the point that he could live off their income. So he learned one of the great financial lessons of life: *security is not in a salary, even if the salary is a fat one.*

After months of confinement in the hospital he left, never to return to work for someone else. He started his own business. Within two years, he had made hundreds of thousands of dollars, which he socked away into income-producing investments that generated enough income so that if he were ever bedridden again he wouldn't have to worry where the next dollar was coming from.

WHERE NOT TO PUT YOUR MONEY; OR, KEEPING UP WITH THE JONESES

As young kids most of us are taught to save our money. Although it's kind of strange that we were never taught what we were saving our money for, by age sixteen or seventeen we eventually figured out that we wanted an automobile. Dumb! It's dumb because a car is an asset that will almost certainly go down in value. But that doesn't seem to bother most people, because they don't stop to think about it.

After a few years most of us, not satisfied with the car we have, go out and buy another one. Again, dumb! It's amazing to me how most people don't think anything of borrowing $8000 to $10,000, or even $15,000, to buy a new car, but if you suggest to them that they use that same borrowed money as a downpayment on a property or as seed capital to start a new business, they look at you as if you were crazy. To them, borrowing for such an investment seems highly risky, even though they don't hesitate to invest borrowed money in a depreciating asset.

After schooling, the next major event in our lives seems to be getting married. (Some will say that this is also dumb, but I will remain neutral on the point.) The typical young couple begin their married life by renting an apartment and then borrowing money to furnish it. Surely they must have furniture just like Mom and Dad's—and have it they will (at 24% or 36%). Dumb! They've bought an asset that will go down in value. Then come children and additional expenses. The couple begin to be burdened with debt, and, typically, at some point in the mid- or late twenties, they will swear off debt, seeing it as the ogre that caused all their problems.

Of course, debt was not the cause of the problem. The cause was debt incurred by buying the wrong kinds of assets. If they had bought assets that had even held their value, with their borrowed money they would by now at least have a reasonable net worth.

The couple try hard to get out of debt and stay out, but with all their friends taking exotic vacations, and a few of them buying a week or two time share in some exotic place, it is easy for them to get sidetracked and break their commitment. So almost every step of their way, they are buying the wrong kind of asset. Whether it is a time-share condominium, a ski cabin, or a beach house, a new car or furniture, this type of asset consistently deteriorates. Sure, you have to have a car—but why not buy a car that will go up in value?

I know that is going against the grain, that it's going against popular opinion. But sometimes it is even fun to do, because you establish yourself as unique. An older car, for example, in great condition, is going to maintain its value and even in some cases appreciate. I bought a 1953 Rolls-Royce a number of years ago and shipped it here from England. In addition to driving it around town for years with great pride and comment, I'm happy to say that the car has now more than doubled in value. And it cost less than an average midsize new car costs today.

Just remember: you *can* break out of the debt trap and make your money, borrowed or not, work for you.

COURAGE FOR CASH

People don't have cash because they don't have courage. I know most people think they don't have cash because they don't make enough to cover all their bills. But that answer doesn't make sense. People without courage and commitment always tend to spend more than they bring in. It doesn't matter if they are making $10,000 or $50,000 or $100,000. They still outspend their income. It's a lot easier to follow the crowd and buy the second or third car or take the Hawaiian vacation when they can't afford it. No one wants to be called stingy, and it's tough enough to say no when you are asked for donations. And, after all, everyone buys new clothes for the holidays. But you are going to have to postpone gratification if you want to accumulate cash.

You are going to have to develop a lot of courage. Enough courage to rely on yourself to do things even though you will be criticized for them. Courage to learn from the consequences of all your choices. If you follow the courage guidelines and remain committed to your goals, you will have enough cash to buy five Rolls-Royces and take ten trips to Hawaii every year if that is what you choose to do.

BASIC NINTH-GRADE MATH REQUIRED

A thorough review of basic mathematics will save you a great deal of time in pursuing financial goals. Larry Rosenberg of

Denver, Colorado, the man who probably influenced me most when I started buying property, told me that all it took to make a million dollars via real estate or income-producing properties was to understand ninth-grade math. The more I studied, the more I saw how right he was.

One of the first things you need to understand is the simple but dramatically effective concept of compounding money, which is return upon return upon return. Banks advertise for you to bring your money to them so you can enjoy compounding your cash at 9%, 10%, 11%, or 15%, whatever the going rate happens to be. Mathematically, that is very simple to understand if you know how to multiply.

The real intrigue comes when you compound your money at much higher rates—50% or 100%, or even more—which is not only possible but is done on a regular basis by thousands of people.

The real key is not how much money you start with, but at what rates you can compound what little money you have, and how much time you have to compound that money. Use of the compounding principle makes it simple to make a million dollars before you are too old to enjoy it.

WISE WORK

In order to benefit from the compounding principle, you are going to have to push yourself to use your time more effectively and efficiently. Here is the key: *To make a million workwise, do "wise work."* You can even cut your hours drastically if you make each hour more effective.

Think about the times in your life when you have had to leave town for some reason, a trip for vacation or business. Before that trip you became very efficient, making long lists of things that had to be done before you went. You were in a time bind, so you got the job done. Chances are, by the time you were ready to leave, your desk had never been so clear.

Work is like gas: it will expand to take up as much space as you will allow. Though gas will disseminate to fill up a room, it can also be compressed into a very tiny cylinder. Give work your whole day and it takes up every minute. If you pace or push yourself, the same amount of work will take only the time you choose to allot.

YOU INHERITED 613,000 THE DAY YOU WERE BORN

The average man born in America inherited 613,200. The average woman, more—674,520. Before you get all excited wondering where your inheritance of over a half million is, know that it is your normal life expectancy in hours in the United States. Those hours happen to be the most precious asset that any one of us possesses. Unfortunately, none of us can go back and relive the time that has already gone by. But we can make the most of what we have now and what we will have in the future.

Here are some techniques for stretching the few hours that each of us possesses:

- If you know what you want, go after it and don't let other people sidetrack you with things that don't matter to you.
- Prioritize everything—do the most important things first. I use an alphabetical system, putting As by those items on my list that are most important that day, Bs by the next most important things to accomplish, and Cs by things that are not high-priority items.

  My As are not exclusively financial either. My family and friends are definitely a top A priority; nothing is more important. All the money in the entire world, and all the fame, are worthless unless you have loved ones and friends with whom to share.
- Stretch time by systems. I find that the most successful people in the world are list makers. They have lists for everything. Lists of friends, lists of relatives, lists of phone numbers and business acquaintances, lists of businesses, lists of tennis partners, lists of hotels around the world they like to stay in. They use these lists religiously and faithfully.

ADVERTISING

All people on their way to the top have to be interested in saving time. Well thought-out advertising in the right media can quickly save you thousands of hours and net a great deal of money as a result. Years ago, when I was a stockbroker, I quickly figured out that if I could talk to ten people at once, rather than just one, I could be much more efficient and consequently much more dollar-effective. I was frustrated by the fact that as an individual stockbroker I could not do my own advertising. I used to look at the total circulation of newspapers and magazines and be frustrated knowing that I wasn't talking to all these hundreds of thousands of people, as I could be. When I finally got out of the stock-brokerage business, I quickly put my thoughts and ideas to work by creating the best possible ads I could. Ads that would grab people's attention. Ads that motivated them to pick up the phone and call me or clip a coupon and write to me.

LEARN TO SAY NO

The next time-saving device is to learn to say no without guilt. Almost all of us were taught as kids that it wasn't polite to turn down requests for our time in various community and church projects. What many of us fail to see is that institutions and individuals often manipulate us by playing on our guilt.

One way to say no without feeling guilty is to try to imagine yourself with a very limited amount of time left in your life. If, for example, you had only six months to live, would you do some of the things you are presently doing? Would you accept assignments from institutions in which you have no interest?

Live your dreams—not someone else's. Constantly tell yourself that. You will find it easier to turn down requests for your time with this in mind because you know that the goals you have set for yourself are very important. By staying on track to reach those goals, you and your family and loved ones will be better off.

Constantly consider the relevance of all you undertake to do. Consider where it is taking you. Consider what time it is taking from you. If you do, I think you will find yourself being able to say no without a second thought.

5

COPYING SUCCESS WITHOUT CHEATING

CREATIVE IMITATION/ADAPTATION

Copy somebody exactly and you might get sued, but copy somebody with your personal touch and you could make a million dollars.

Most people copy, but few people admit it. We all want the world to think that we generate original ideas. Only a secure person is totally at ease with learning from others. People who value learning from the past and from contemporaries purposely set out to study and to observe others and their successes, then go about duplicating them in their own style so that their contribution becomes unique. An exact copy usually doesn't work and could be the cause of a lawsuit. And sometimes you don't need to make changes at all. Fortunes are made weekly by people who merely take a concept, a product, or a service they saw in one market to a new market. They see something being done in one city and say, "Hey, that'll work in my town." If you try to copy somebody exactly in the same market, people will often regard it as a ripoff and will not pay the price that they would to the originator of the idea or product.

A business associate of mine, William Oliver Parry III, freely admits that he copies all the time. He adds to what he sees and he improves it, making changes here and there. Bill is in the building business as a developer and contractor. Most of his good ideas come from Southern California, where they seem to be the innovators, at least in the home-building business. He looks at companies to see which new patterns, designs, and projects are popular and accepted by the public. Then he applies what he sees to different states and cities throughout the US. Bill says, "A person has to be pretty slow, lazy or dull, not to be very successful by observing and then doing what is working for others." The trick is to take "normally unrelated" items, ideas, products, words, or contents and put them together in a way a little different from anyone else. If you can do that you'll earn yourself the label of creative genius.

LEARNING FROM THE WORLDWIDE COPYCATS

The Japanese lost the war, but they are winning all the battles now. The Japanese are beating the socks off all of us almost every day. The irony is that we gave them the pattern. Show me a Japanese businessman touring our farms, factories, offices, and warehouses, and I'll show you two Yashicas, a Pentax, Minolta, and a Nikon hanging around his neck, loaded with 36-exposure film in each camera. With one single trip to the United States, enterprising Japanese business people can take back to their country twenty or thirty years' of research, study, and testing. Daily they are taking back memories and impressions stored in their minds, enough film exposed to the right pictures, and stacks of magazines and newspapers that tell it all.

HOW TO COPY THE COPYCATS

It may sound as though I am being critical of the Japanese, but nothing could be further from the truth. I have the greatest admiration for them and for anyone else who uses his head and takes the time to observe what others are doing and who can duplicate their efforts with their own twist.

You can do the same thing the Japanese are doing. They don't have a corner on that market. They cannot patent or copyright their copycat capers. You can do exactly the same thing. It takes time and effort, yes. But mostly it takes good powers of observation and keen awareness.

BE ALL EYES

If you are going to copy someone's success, make sure you know exactly *what* they are doing. Not what it *appears* they are doing. It takes time and effort to study and to unveil those kinds of details.

Ray Kroc was selling milkshake mixers when he noticed the McDonald brothers' hamburger stand in San Bernardino was generating a lot of interest. He made it a point to observe every detail of their successful single operation, bought them out, and chained golden arches around the world. The basic fast-foods franchise idea has a variety of applications as well as much successful product-on-product competition.

Ray Kroc definitely copied somebody else's idea. And not only that, the hamburger itself, his basic product, was not exactly a new invention. He just began marketing it in a different way. As he said, "I didn't invent the hamburger, I just took it more seriously than anyone else."

CASH FROM COOKIES

Normally a chocolate chip cookie is not very exciting. Most of us have eaten dozens. But Debbie Fields, the exuberant president of Mrs. Fields Cookies, saw the chocolate chip in a different way. She decided to make the best chocolate chip cookie in the business. She used real butter, real chocolate, real vanilla. Besides that, she put more chocolate and goodies than flour into her cookies. Then she copied a highly successful marketing plan and began selling cookies, just as Ray Kroc did selling hamburgers. She offered the best cookie going and did it with fast, friendly service. She opened her first cookie shop in Palo Alto, California, near Stanford University. She sold $200,000 worth of cookies the first year. Five years later, she sold more than $30 million in a single year. And get this: she is only twenty-six years old!

Just like the hamburger people or the chefs at Benihana's, she decided to bake the cookies right there in front of your eyes. Yes, she copied other people, but she did it with her own flair and her own personality and nobody would dare call her a ripoff.

She not only duplicated the fast-food business, she borrowed some management concepts from the Japanese. (After all, turnaround is fair play, isn't it?) What did she borrow? The concept of decision from the bottom up, getting feedback from employees first. Second, respect for people, both employees and customers. And lastly, their motto, which is first, high quality; second, friendly service; and third, fast service.

ALL CREATIVITY IS NOT COPYING: RELATING ODDITIES

Paul J. Meyer, founder and president of Success Motivation Institute, based in Waco, Texas, came from a less-than-affluent family. But he had a brilliant father who taught his son the concept of relating the normally unrelated. He taught him that if he wanted to succeed, all he had to do was look around and put two things together that normally aren't together. It took Paul years to get started, but when he did, nothing could stop him.

From his insurance business experience Paul Meyer knew a lot about selling. Paul also knew a lot about motivation. He knew when to motivate people and how to motivate people. Just prior to 1960, music was beginning to be introduced on cassette tapes rather than on records. It seemed like the thing of the future. At that time, only music was available on cassette tapes. By drawing from the philosophy of his father, Paul Meyer reasoned that information on goal-setting and salesmanship techniques could be put on tapes. At least he thought they could, even though no one had done it. But why not? He was relating the unrelated, bringing two things together that really didn't seem to fit *at the time*.

Paul Meyer went beyond the conventional wisdom. He has subsquently built an eighty-million-dollar company from that idea. If you think that's just a fluke, think again. Paul Meyer's father taught Paul's brother, Karl, the same philosophy. What did Karl do? Well, Karl was in the pool business and was making wood diving boards. One day Paul and Karl noticed the range of things being made of fiberglass. They reasoned that they could make a diving board out of fiberglass. Thus Karl Meyer came up with the first fiberglass diving board and sold thousands.

You see, creativity is not usually coming up with something totally new, it is combining two things that are already known to make something that is new and marketable.

POPCORN CAN EAT WEEDS

Back in the early 1970s, George Ballas, an owner of a dance studio in Houston, was faced with a very frustrating problem. Being a meticulous man, Ballas was anxious to keep his lawn neatly trimmed. But the grass around some oak tree roots had him stumped. There was no way to keep that grass cut unless it was done by hand. Since his house was on a bayou, anyone doing hand trimming was likely to run across a copperhead or two crawling around in the weeds.

This trimming problem continued to plague Ballas for several years. Then one day at an automatic car wash, he had a brainstorm. He became intrigued by the whirling bristles of nylon that spun along the top and sides of his car. He noticed how the bristles cleaned without damaging the car and thought about the grass that had grown so close to the tree trunks that conventional lawnmowers can't touch. He rushed back to his house with an idea in mind.

From his trash bin he retrieved a discarded popcorn can, punched holes in it, and threaded the holes with nylon fishing line. He then removed the metal blade from his lawn edger, bolted the popcorn can contraption to the long handle, and started it.

It made a racket, but it ripped up the turf and tore away the grass without damaging the tree roots, which is what he wanted to accomplish.

Ballas later named his device the "Weed Eater." He claims his was the first practical device that eliminated the back-breaking work of hand-cutting weeds and overgrown grass around all those pesty places such as fences, stones, and tree roots. Another key advantage of his new trimmer was the safety factor, since nylon line will not cut the skin like a conventional metal blade.

Ballas spent about $10,000 developing his popcorn-can contraption. The first model weighed thirty pounds, was powered by a small gasoline engine, and sold commercially for about $300.

When the first Weed Eater was perfected, he found no one was interested. Distributors didn't want to carry it because they thought it was overpriced and too awkward to handle. He tried to interest turf-equipment companies, golf clubs, country clubs, wholesalers, and highway departments. Finally, in frustration, he forged ahead on his own, convinced that his invention was the lawn tool of the future.

Ballas became the proverbial traveling salesman, selling the trimmer door to door from the trunk of his car. After some time, he pulled together enough money for advertising. He and his son shot some film commercials of him using the Weed Eater. Then he bought $12,000 worth of commercial air time on a local television station. Word spread quickly and sales took off.

One day a sixty-year-old woman wanted to buy a string trimmer but found it too cumbersome. Ballas soon came out with a lightweight model that was electrically powered. Sales continued to grow at a phenomenal rate.

Even though Ballas applied for a patent on his invention, other manufacturers began to see the potential in the product and jumped on the bandwagon. Soon Sears, Black & Decker, and Toro had entered the market, and it became clear that the industry was established.

Ballas sold Weed Eater, Inc., to Emerson Electric Co. in 1977. Since that time, Weed Eater has remained the number-one string trimmer in the world.

FROM THEORY TO PRACTICE

By now you're probably anxious to know what specific actions you can take to achieve financial freedom or independence and to reach your goal before it's too late to enjoy it. The answer, and probably the single biggest key to financial success, is finding and negotiating with the "motivated seller." He can make you rich almost overnight if you find him.

6

MOTIVATED SELLERS WILL LINE YOUR POCKETS WITH CASH

THE SUPER KEY TO SUCCESS

Analyzing my own successes and the successes of others shows conclusively that finding and dealing with motivated sellers will make you rich in the shortest amount of time. Someone who is super motivated to sell something suffers from a sort of temporary insanity. If, for some reason, he or she is "down" on a property or asset, reason seems to fly out the window and emotion takes over. Stop and think of your own actions. Have you ever owned a car that you became totally disenchanted with—the water pump goes out one week, three weeks later it's the distributor or the battery? There's a dent in the side, and then the speedometer cable goes, or one of the headlights, so you finally reach a point at which you are totally fed up. You think, "What a piece of junk! I've got to get rid of this garbage heap. It's falling apart. What I need is a new car." The instant you think these thoughts you cease to be objective. Your emotions say the old car is nearly worthless. You unknowingly have just set the perfect stage for someone to make a quick and easy profit, even if it's only a few hundred dollars. And so you say, "So, what's a few hundred dollars?" But the same thing happens with hundred-thousand-dollar and million-dollar properties.

2½% DOWN: WHAT A DUMB OFFER

Several years ago I decided to buy a new home. I found the ideal home, complete with tennis courts, swimming pool, and almost three acres in a beautifully wooded area. I bought it and moved in. So there I sat with two homes. I paid $260,000 for the new home and I was trying to sell the old one, which cost $55,000, for $100,000. I was making payments on both, $1550 a month on the second home and $550 on the old one. For a month, nothing happened. I hadn't received a single offer on the property that I was trying to sell. Two months. Then three months. Nothing. During the fourth month some kids broke in and did several hundred dollars' worth of damage. I fixed the damage only to have the FOR SALE sign stolen about every other week. As the summer grew hotter, the lawn started to burn up and I had to make many trips to the property to water it.

Well, I was rapidly becoming a motivated seller. I was sick and tired of the property. I just wanted to get rid of it. Finally, in the seventh month a young man made me the following offer: $2500 down. Remember, the price was $100,000, so his downpayment was only 2½%. He did offer me full purchase price, but his monthly payment to me would be only $450 whereas mine was $550 a month. He wanted me to "carry it" on a so-called wraparound whereby I would be putting out $100 each month to make up the difference between his payment and what I owed the bank. What a ridiculous, dumb offer! But I was dumber than he was. I took it. Why did I take it? Because I was a motivated seller.

WHEN ARE PEOPLE TRANSFORMED INTO MOTIVATED SELLERS?

Do you think that I would have taken that same offer within two or three weeks of listing the property for sale? Of course I wouldn't have. What about after two or three months? Probably not. When did I become a motivated seller? I can't really pinpoint the exact moment I was transformed into a motivated seller, but I was transformed by the time the low offer was made.

It was a great experience because it taught me what a motivated seller thinks about when he has a property that he is emotionally down on. Oh, I could afford the payments on both houses, but I didn't like making both. I started to project in my mind that this could go on forever. Knowing that it was costing me $6600 a year, I became very concerned. I had projected far into the future what it was costing me. I thought I would continue to have the problems of vandalism, dying lawns, and other nuisances. I thought I was pouring money down a rat-hole. I worried that the economy was getting worse and might collapse. I was motivated to sell. With these worries and negative thoughts rumbling around in my head, his offer looked good. It was a way to get out of my problem right now.

I look back and see I should have waited. At the time it seemed like a good enough deal. Consequently, someone else got a super deal—and I learned what motivated sellers think about.

If you are in the right place at the right time, you can take advantage of the eagerness of motivated sellers and pick up $50,000 to $100,000 in one fell swoop. With that kind of money on the line, it is well worth your time to scout out the motivated seller.

A BEGINNER MAKES $100,000 ON HIS FIRST DEAL. WHY? YOU GUESSED IT. A MOTIVATED SELLER

Dick Hamilton, of Indianapolis, didn't know much about buying properties, but he did know about the motivated seller from reading just one book. He says in his case ignorance was bliss. He could really see that some people are at times extremely motivated to sell their property, so he went about to capitalize on that understanding. Even though Dick didn't fully understand the mechanics of buying, selling, or managing property, he forged ahead.

When Dick Hamilton found an eighty-year-old gentleman who owned a forty-eight-unit apartment building that had thirty-two vacancies, he knew he had found a motivated seller. Besides that, the man lived in Florida and had hired a local company to manage his property. (Obviously they weren't managing the property very well with thirty-two vacancies.) Knowing the man had headaches with the property and wanted to get rid of it, Dick offered $100,000 total price on the property, which was worth $200,000.

That's right, he offered half of the true value of the property. He told the seller he would give him $50,000 at the time of closing and that the balance of $50,000 would be paid over a five-year period with a 10% interest rate on a ten-year amortization, which worked out to be an average payment of $833 a month, with a balloon payment after the fifth year. (Amortization is spreading payments out to keep them and interest rates lower each month. That is, over ten (or thirty) years, even though you have agreed to make the balloon payment in five years. The balloon payment is a lump sum that pays off the balance owed.)

CRAZY OFFER PRODUCES A MIRACLE

With a crazy offer like that, Dick didn't expect the seller to accept it. He thought the offer would be rejected and at very best he would have to make a counteroffer. But, miracle of miracles, it was accepted exactly as written. Dick couldn't believe it. It seemed too good to be true. But it was. Even though Dick didn't know much about property management, you can believe he learned fast. In a short time he had the vacancies reduced to zero.

Recently he refinanced the property with a new first government loan for $138,500. So not only did he make a $100,000 paper profit, he turned $38,500 of it into cash and still owns the property, currently appraised at $225,000.

You will be interested to know that he didn't even have the $50,000 that he offered as a downpayment. But he quickly got it. How? He simply put a second mortgage on his own residence and got the money from a bank.

I know that many people are reluctant to encumber the very home in which they live. But if you knew that you were buying an asset that was worth $200,000, and your purchase price was only $100,000, it isn't a question of courage to acquire such a super bargain asset. This deal worked because of a motivated seller, a seller so motivated that he would sell his property for half price, a hundred thousand dollars less than it was really worth. That's motivated.

NOT A UNICORN

You might be thinking this story is unusual and that Dick Hamilton was very lucky. But it's not that unusual. Most of the properties I have bought have been purchased from motivated sellers. Many of those purchases have also been "yuk" properties (ones that were rundown and visually undesirable), which has given me a double chance of winning. Years ago, when I first started, I found and negotiated with dozens of motivated sellers on small properties, picking up profits of $5000 and $10,000 per property. I was flabbergasted when I found a motivated seller on a larger property. On paper it looked as if I could make $50,000 on one single deal. I found it hard to believe, but it was true. In fact, I have since found that there are motivated sellers at all levels, from the $10,000 properties to the multimillion-dollar ones. The same applies for all types of businesses.

SOME CAUTIONS

Be sure you know the price you are getting is truly a bargain price. Some people pretend to be motivated sellers when in fact the bargain come-on is a gimmick to get the buyer's attention. Be skeptical when listening to reasons sellers give for selling. Truly motivated sellers don't usually announce that they are motivated. The circumstances generally tell the full story, and the seller tries not to appear to be overeager.

COMPARISON SHOPPING

There is no substitute for spending time to shop around and comparing one asset with another, or one property with another. If you don't do this, you could be offered a super deal and never recognize it for what it is, or you could end up paying too much for a property or business. If you take the time to shop and compare, you will know value when you see it. That helps you know when a seller is truly motivated or just pretending to be. The hours you spend getting to know prices and values will reward you handsomely.

The first time you ever make $50,000 or $100,000 on one deal, in a matter of months, people who know you will call you lucky. That is what they said about me when I ended up buying a very large property for well under the market price.

A "LUCKY" TWO-MILLION-DOLLAR DEAL

I received a phone call one Friday from an obviously motivated seller in Pennsylvania. The numbers that he gave me over the phone were too good to be true. I asked all the necessary questions and the deal still sounded terrific. In fact, it sounded so good that that very day I put an employee on a plane to Pennsylvania. He called me the next day to tell me the apartment complex was as good as it was represented to be. I was so excited I could hardly sit still, and barely slept that night. The numbers indicated that the property was worth at least $700,000 more than I had to pay for it. As a matter of fact, I sold it one year and one month later for more than $2 million cash in my pocket over what I paid for it.

Sound unbelievable? Well, it may sound that way but that is exactly what happened. Who in their right mind would sell a property that is worth so much more than the purchase price? The answer is a super-motivated seller. In fact, there were three motivated sellers. Here is what happened.

The court forced a man into a very illiquid cash position because of his divorce. That man lost the property to the court. The court was now the motivated seller. It had a property that it didn't want, and had to dispose of it. The court, like most government bodies, really didn't know what it was doing.

The court sold the property to an individual investor who had figured what it was really worth, but was trying to finance the property so he wouldn't have to put a single penny of his own money into it. He had given the court a $50,000 deposit to show his good intentions. At the last moment the finance company which had agreed to finance the deal found out that the buyer had no money of his own in the deal, so they quickly withdrew their commitment to finance, leaving the investor in a very bad position. When he called me, he was about to lose $50,000 because he only had three days to come up with financing for the property, and he knew he couldn't get it.

Realizing what the property was worth, I moved fast, so fast I even shocked myself. But I knew that I would be missing out on an easy automatic profit of $700,000 if I didn't come up with the financing, so I was prepared to move heaven and earth to get the money. And after all that, people called me lucky! But anyone can be "lucky" if he or she goes out and takes the time to compare properties to hunt, to find, and to negotiate with motivated sellers.

That is exactly what I did to be sure that the property was worth at least $700,000 more than the asking price. Then with great persistence I was able to come up with the money within three days.

You have heard of people lifting automobiles off trapped children. Well, we also have Superman strength to accomplish nonphysical tasks. *If you are sufficiently motivated, if you know for a fact that you can make a small or large fortune in a very short period of time, then you can do it.*

CLUE YOURSELF TO THE RIGHT ASSETS

You may not be able to come even close to identifying a million-dollar super deal unless you are out there looking for it. If you want to make some huge profits, for heaven's sakes get out of the penny-ante stuff. With the same effort, energy, and time spent looking for super-motivated sellers of dogs and cats, you could look for motivated sellers who own appreciating assets that are worth tens of thousands, or hundreds of thousands, of dollars or even more.

I know a young man who spends countless hours finding motivated sellers of automobiles. He finds them, negotiates an even better price, fixes the cars up, and turns around and sells them, making two or three thousand dollars at the very most on each one. (See Chapter 7 on "How Yuks Can Create Big Bucks.") With that same energy the young man could be making hundreds of thousands of dollars each year on larger deals.

MOTIVATED SELLERS: WHO ARE THEY?

You are no doubt wondering who these motivated sellers are. How can they be identified?

There are many reasons why people are motivated to sell at lower than true value. Here are a few:

- Death
- Divorce
- Relocation
- Getting older
- Seller wants new challenges
- Seller is uninformed
- Seller has a fear of the future
- Seller is tired of managing property
- Problems with tenants or employees

- Physical problems with buildings, plant, equipment
- Market for the product seems to be dropping

FEELINGS OVERRIDE FACTS

You must realize that most of us make the majority of our decisions based on feelings rather than facts. We do listen and digest and react partially because of facts, but under certain circumstances (see the list), feelings tend to override facts. Many people are pushed to the point of saying, "I'm selling it for a much lower price than it is really worth, but I just don't care. I just want out. I want to be done with it!"

ADVANTAGES TO THE BUYER

The list of advantages of buying from motivated sellers include:

- Lower price.
- Possibly no cash outlay now.
- Pay over the long term. (Here you really end up buying the asset with the seller's own cash, which is generated from the asset.)
- All terms—the length of time it takes to pay off the asset, the amount down, the price of the asset, and, most important, the interest rate that you will be paying on the balance—are all negotiable.

HOW TO RECOGNIZE THE MOTIVATED SELLER

There are two things that are normally a dead giveaway in identifying a motivated seller. The first one is the seller: what he does, what he says, and how he acts. The second is his property or business and what it looks like.

Does he talk negatively about the asset that he is trying to sell, or make disparaging remarks about the physical aspects, the tenants or employees? If so, then that should raise a red flag in your mind. He might be motivated.

If he talks about how bad the market for his product is or how slowly things are selling, that is a sign. If he is fed up with his business or buildings, or if he is worried about the future, that is a sign of a motivated seller. Or possibly his profit margins are starting to narrow. It is a sign if he talks about recession or depression. If he doesn't talk about any of the above items, ask questions to pull it out of him: "What do you think is going to happen to the economy?", you might ask. Or: "Isn't it a shame the way profit margins are being squeezed now." Or: "Boy, the cost of property taxes and operating expenses are just about more than anybody can take these days!" Asking these questions and then listening carefully to the answers can give you a clue to his or her level of motivation. Be sure to listen hard to his answers.

After looking at him, look at the property or the company he owns. What does it look like? Is it run-down; is it in bad need of repairs? Are there lots of vacancies? Are there problems with the employees? Many of these things are very obvious; they just take time to observe. Is the business run in a neat, organized way? Or are there papers strewn every which way in a disorganized mess? Again, you can probe if he or she doesn't volunteer the information. Ask questions such as, "It's really a shame that they don't build buildings like they used to." Here you are attacking the building, not the owner personally, so he won't get defensive. Or the old catch-all statement, "You just can't get good help these days, can you?" Or: "Don't you find it hard to find good, stable, hardworking employees?" Again listen to his answers.

HOW TO SMOKE OUT A MOTIVATED SELLER

Finding a motivated seller is not as difficult as you think, but you really do have to make it happen. *You can't sit home and expect deals to come looking for you.* You need to be out in the marketplace, asking questions, asking for referrals, telling people what you are doing and asking them to spread the word. There might be a perfect purchase for you out there somewhere, with a motivated seller who would love to sell at exactly your price and terms, but if you never meet the seller you will never make the deal.

Fortunately there are some methods that help you dig up motivated sellers with relatively little time expenditure on your part.

THE SHOTGUN METHOD

The shotgun method is quite simple in concept but it does take some work. The results, however, can be phenomenal, because you can reach so many people in a relatively short period of time. A twenty-gauge shotgun has the ability to bring down a bird more easily than a rifle because of the hundreds of BBs that are released. It only takes one or two for success. Similarly, the shotgun method is a matter of numbers. Send out enough offers and you're bound to win.

The shotgun approach can be used when you are buying or selling any type of asset. When most people apply for a job or a loan, they approach just one bank or employer, fill out an application, and then wait to find out the results. At the end of the waiting period, which can be five or six weeks, they have to start all over again if they are turned down. If, however, they were smart enough to use a shotgun approach, applying for jobs or loans at six or so places, they might get turned down on two or three, or even five, but are accepted by one and end up a winner—plus having saved all that time and anxiety.

When you look for motivated sellers, why not go with a shotgun approach? For example, if you are looking to buy a small business through a business broker, write the same letter to twenty or thirty brokers at the same time. If you are buying an office building or shopping center or apartment complex in a nearby town, write to *all* the brokers. For that matter, write to all the apartment owners in the town, if it is not too big a town. If you do this, you will save a lot of time, which, of course, is the most precious thing that you and I possess.

If 80% of the business brokers are not interested in you or haven't got what you want to buy, that's okay, because the other 20% will. Ditto for real estate brokers and/or owners of whatever kind of asset you are trying to buy.

The second way to use the shotgun method, a way specifically designed to smoke out the motivated seller, is by sending dozens of letters with an actual written offer for the asset. Since you are looking for the motivated seller, your offer will be very low. For example, you may offer 20% to 30% lower than the asking price for the asset. Your offer of cash out of pocket should also be very low, as well as all the other terms of the offer. In fact, you may wish to offer nothing down at all. *The point is to try to smoke out the motivated seller.* If you send out one hundred low offers, more than 90% will come back marked not acceptable. (Of course, some of them won't even come back because your offer is so low.) But you are looking for the motivated seller, and since he is not sitting out there with an "M" branded on his forehead, you have to find him through the most effective and efficient way that you can. This way works. I know, because many people have used it successfully. In fact, one major merger firm in New York City uses this as its primary method of soliciting medium- and small-sized corporations that need or want to be sold.

REFERRAL METHODS

I rarely go to a movie that hasn't been praised to me. Before I waste my time sitting in a theater, I need to talk to someone who has seen it to get his or her opinion. Word of mouth is the best, the least expensive, and the most powerful advertising that any company can hope to have.

In your quest for financial independence and freedom, a good, well-oiled, well-organized referral system can work wonders and is critical to your success, since your time is so limited. If you tell ten friends that you are looking for a certain type of distressed asset, give them some particulars, and ask them to talk to at least five of their friends, you will have contacted sixty people in short order.

You should also use this technique in trying to sell any of your appreciating assets. In fact, I use this method when trying to find partners for ventures. I alter the method slightly by calling ten friends and asking them for a list of ten people by name and phone number. I specifically ask the question, "Who do you think the ten most successful, upcoming young people in the city are?"

When I ask specific questions like this I get specific answers. If, on the other hand, I were to call a friend and say, "Listen, do you know some successful people in this town? If you can think of their names why don't you give me a call sometime?", I would get an answer of, "Sure, I'll call you if I can think of somebody. Good-bye." Click. Hang up. And that would be the end of that. My friend would never call. But when I specifically ask for a certain number of friends, (three, five, or ten), using the right words so that it is not a threat to them or to their friendships, then I almost always get results. When I call these people, I use the friend's name as the person who referred me to them. Like magic, I get a warm welcome from these people.

FORECLOSURES

It is safe to say that anyone who has had a property foreclosed qualifies as a motivated seller. An investor who has an under-standing of the foreclosure process can often buy real estate far below market prices. Prudent use of investment dollars in this fascinating market can create excellent returns. Though lenders usually foreclose on less than 1% of their outstanding mortgage loans, the great volume of mortgages makes even this small percentage meaningful.

TYPES OF FORECLOSURES

There are two types of foreclosures in this country: "strict foreclosure" and "foreclosure by sale." Few states presently have strict foreclosure procedures. In those states the bor-rower loses his or her title to the property unless the lender is paid in full by a court-designated date. The time allowed the borrower is in direct proportion to his or her equity in the prop-erty; that is, the fair market value of the property (as deter-mined by one or more court-appointed appraisers) less claims against it, such as mortgages, taxes, and other liens. The more equity in the property the borrower has, the more time the court will give the borrower to pay off the delinquent mortgage.

The most common type of foreclosure is foreclosure by sale. Under this procedure the property is sold to the highest bidder at a court-supervised public auction. The proceeds of the sale are applied to all claims against the property and any funds left over are paid to the borrower.

ONLY ONE BIDDER

Often at public auctions of real estate the only bidder present is a representative of the lender whose mortgage is being fore-closed. The lender's representative bids an amount sufficient to pay off the lender. If there are no other bidders, the lender winds up owning the property. Usually the lender thereafter at-tempts to sell the property at fair market value.

Let's look at a hypothetical case. Borrower Jones buys a property for $80,000 and pays $60,000 of the purchase price with the proceeds of a mortgage loan from Dollar Bank. Sev-eral years later the property is worth $100,000 with a mort-gage balance of $50,000. Jones then fails to make payments and Dollar Bank forecloses. Attorney fees, court costs, appraisal fees, accrued interest, and unpaid real estate taxes total $5000. Dollar Bank needs $55,000 in order to avoid a loss.

If the bank were the only bidder at a public auction, it could own a $100,000 property for $55,000. Instances of this sort may be rare but are not unheard of. Jones would lose the property and be paid nothing. An investor could bid $60,000 or $75,000 at such an auction and get a bargain. Jones then might at least realize a few thousand dollars for his equity instead of zero. Even on those occasions where several bidders compete at a public auction, the successful bidder usually makes a very good deal.

AN ATTRACTIVE MARKET

How does the investor involve himself in this active and attractive market? A real estate broker has at his or her fingertips the most efficient sources of information concerning pendency of foreclosure actions. Public auctions of real estate are announced and advertised in designated media with which the broker is familiar. The broker often checks public records to get early leads. He or she keeps in close contact with the attorneys and bankers who are central to this market.

Get to know and develop a rapport with an experienced, well-qualified broker. If the broker is convinced you are serious, you might negotiate an arrangement whereby the broker gathers data for you about foreclosure sales in your area of interest for little or no fee. You could offer to list the properties you acquire through his or her efforts with the broker, for lease or resale at current market prices, so the broker could end up making some good on his arrangement with you. Innovative thinking coupled with prudence can earn rich rewards in this exciting and often overlooked market.

YOU MAKE IT HAPPEN

All the techniques in the world won't help unless you make it happen. There is an amazing synergistic effect once you get started. It may seem slow at first, but once you get moving, things will begin to snowball. Referrals and answers to offers and letters you wrote weeks and months before using the

7

HOW YUKS CAN CREATE BIG BUCKS

CHANGING A TACKY DUMP INTO A SWISS CHALET

I really couldn't believe what I saw. A few years ago while driving down a street in Salt Lake City, I glanced over at a little white house (maybe a thousand square feet at the most) and just about drove off the road. The formerly grungy house had been completely transformed. Instead of a tacky little house complete with cluttered yard, worn grass, and garbage cans by the porch, I saw a cute, Swiss chalet-like cottage. The change was so stunning that I pulled over to stop and stare. At first glance it seemed that someone had spent a ton of dough making the property shine. Upon closer inspection, I found that the changes made on the outside of the property were quite inexpensive. The dirt had been covered up by a fresh coat of paint, and shutters with decorative patterns had been placed on either side of the windows. The front yard had been resodded and a few nice shrubs placed on either side of the porch. The garbage cans had been moved from the front yard to the back. For frosting, a white picket fence had been put along the front of the yard. One other conspicuous difference was a FOR SALE sign prominently displayed.

I was amazed at the change, but even more amazed at my reaction to the change. I had for years been in the business of buying properties that needed fixing up and reselling after some work or refinancing at very substantial profits. Prior to stopping, I considered myself very successful at what I did.

The shocking part of this experience was my first reaction, which was, "What a cute little house. It's absolutely darling. I ought to buy it."

Talk about dumb. Really dumb. Here I am in the business of cleaning up other people's messes to create value for turnaround, and profiting from that cleanup and turnaround, and I was almost tricked into buying a property that had already been fixed up.

PRETTY BRINGS TOP DOLLAR

It was a great experience for me because it taught me the valuable lesson that almost anyone would rather buy property that is nice or new or all fixed up; and they will usually pay a premium for it. Ponder that. Wouldn't you rather buy something on which the work has already been done? Something that looks neat and tidy and pretty? I found out that I would.

The problem is that most people don't have a vision of what can be done with tacky-looking, beat-up properties. By the way, such properties include a lot more than income-producing properties, apartment buildings, homes, shopping centers, office buildings, and the like. They include all types of assets, even corporations or small businesses, various kinds of rare land, and even automobiles.

THERE'S BIG BUCKS IN THE YUKS

Even if you don't have the vision to see what can be done with the property to dramatically increase its value, there are people you can easily hire, or even borrow without pay, to help you see what improvements can be made.

By now you probably have figured out what a yuk is. Whenever you see one you should check it out. It's obvious why yuks will make you big bucks. And I mean big.

A yuk is a property that quickly brings forth the response, "Oh, yuk! Look at *that* place," when you drive by. A junky-looking property usually tells you several things quite quickly that can translate into some very large profits for you. First, it usually says that the owner doesn't care about the property. Second, he or she is a lazy owner. Third, he has no imagination of what could be done, or, fourth, he has no money to do it. The bottom line of this is that the owner of a yuk is probably a motivated seller. The property is probably draining him if not financially, then at least mentally and emotionally and probably both.

A YUK SANDWICH SHOP

You can spot a yuk business from the way it is run. Everything from the condition of the business office and/or showroom, store, company cars and trucks, and the general response of the business in dealing with the public shows it. Each of us bumps into businesses like this almost every day.

Years ago, while training to be a stockbroker in Manhattan, I went to lunch every day on one of the upper floors of a large office building at a sandwich shop for building employees. Each day, standing in the long line, I became more amazed by this sloppily run, totally inefficient business. It wasn't that their sandwiches were poor—in fact, they were delicious! But their efficiency factor was absolutely dreadful. The waiting time in line for the sandwiches was sometimes a full thirty-five minutes. With only an hour for lunch, we often would opt for another place to eat even though it was more expensive.

To me, the solution to the problem in the sandwich shop was simple. Their system was that as each customer stepped to the counter to order his sandwich, it was "custom-built" right there in front of him by one of three employees. This customizing might have appealed to many customers, but by building the sandwiches prior to the crowd coming in for lunch, I am sure that the number of customers lost would not have come close to the number gained because of shorter lines. The sandwich shop's troubles could also have been easily resolved by upping the price in order to shorten the line, which would have maximized profits, too.

YUKS HAVE POTENTIAL

The condition of the run-down property or poorly run business should also quickly tell you something else, something quite obvious. It has potential for improvement. That improvement can mean great profits for you. You see, buying a new or nearly new property, or a very well run business, leaves no room for dramatic increases in the value because it is already close to the maximum value.

Most people have no idea how much money is being made every day by thousands of courageous men and women. It takes courage. Don't forget it. It takes courage and smarts to recognize the great potential in the yuks and super yuks. One of the purposes of this chapter is to point out the potential profits and to show you the relatively simple ways to take advantage of these properties.

THE HUNDRED-DOLLAR-ARCHITECT TRICK

I am not particularly good at recognizing what can be done to the outside of a building to make it look better or how to make a building that is thirty years old look "new." But there are others who are good at that. Even though I have considerable assets, I don't like to spend thousands of dollars on professional opinions about what exactly can be done with a building. With this background information, let me tell you about the hundred-dollar architect.

THE APARTMENT THAT WANTED TO BE A MOTEL

Most architects are expensive, very expensive, and I knew that, but I had a big problem. The problem was an apartment complex that was in absolutely terrible shape. The buildings were more than twenty years old and they looked it. One local writer said that the apartment building looked as if it had always wanted to be a motel when it grew up. The building also had over 120 broken windows.

There were kicked-in doors and carpets that were so rotten that if you tried to vacuum them, the entire carpet would end up inside the vacuum cleaner. This was topped off by a 76% vacancy. The twenty-four tenants in the building were strictly losers. We had everything from pushers to prostitutes. We had drug users, fencing operations, winos and weirdos—and the tenants went downhill from there. One of my property managers told me that it was a hopeless case, claiming that you can't polish a rotten apple.

I was almost at the point of believing that statement, but I took the time to do something that everyone needs to do if they want to profit handsomely from yuk properties. I took time to do some heavy thinking along with some concentrated observing. After spending more than an hour driving around the property, stopping at various points and looking at the building, I finally determined that the biggest problem was that the entrance to the building was on a major industrial street. The property was designed to have one-way traffic through the complex with the exit on a side street. The traffic was great for exposure, but who wants to live in an industrial area?

EUREKA—I ALMOST HAD THE ANSWER

Once I decided what the major problem was, I continued to observe and drive around the complex, getting out of my car frequently. Finally, I drove around the block to a residential street that was contiguous to the back of my property. I noticed that two properties—small apartment buildings that adjoined my property on the back side—were for sale. When I noticed that the buildings had a driveway between them, I thought I had an answer to my problems. I would buy the two properties behind the complex and use the driveway between them as the entrance to my apartment building in the back. But I soon discovered to my great disappointment that there was not enough space between the two buildings for cars to enter.

HOW COULD I BE SO DUMB AS NOT TO SEE THE OBVIOUS?

As I drove to the exit side of the building, it suddenly hit me. Why not make the exit the entrance and the entrance the exit? The exit emptied onto a side street in a residential area.

The only reason I have gone to this length to give you the details of what I thought and what I wanted to do and what I ended up doing is to make the point that many times our creative ideas take a bit of thinking through before we come up with what seems obvious after the fact. When I look back now and see the entrance where the exit used to be, I mentally kick myself for being dumb enough not to see the solution right from the beginning. The funny thing is that the many other people who had looked at the building (including professionals) never suggested that possibility either.

All of us seemed to be blind to simple changes. But I have repeatedly found that we can regain our vision if we take enough time to think hard and to be good observers. In this one particular case the thinking and observing paid me more than a million dollars.

But my problems weren't over. I knew I had to do something with the exterior of the buildings to attract the kind of tenants I wanted. I had no idea what to do about the elongated look of each of the motel-like buildings. I reasoned that there were people who could possibly give me answers to the question. That's where the hundred-dollar architect enters the picture.

LUNCH AT MCDONALD'S

Not wanting to spend a large sum on architects just for ideas, I called an architect friend of mine and asked him if he'd like to go to lunch. He agreed. After I took him to McDonald's (I told you I was on a budget), we drove by the building and I casually mentioned that I owned it and asked him if he had some ideas about what could be done to make the building look more in tune with the times. He said he thought he and some of the people on his staff might be able to come up with some changes. Of course, I didn't leave our deal that open-ended. I told him to go ahead and see what he could come up with, but that the budget was only a hundred dollars. I said I knew that it wasn't much, but that was all I had to work with on this particular project. I emphasized to him that I just wanted some sketches—whatever a hundred dollars would buy.

To my surprise and delight, about ten days later he brought me the "sketches." He and his staff had come up with drawing after drawing of different inexpensive possibilities of what could be done with the front of the buildings. I had received even more value than I expected. More important, those drawings instantly made me sure that the project would be a huge financial success.

I finally chose a set of drawings that called for some cedar siding placed horizontally on the first and second floors with a four-foot-wide cedar strip that ran vertically up the two stories, spaced every forty feet or so. I rewarded the architect's good work and efforts by letting him do the detail drawings from which we would build. In addition to the trim, we made other minor changes that made a major difference.

- We tore out some of the old-looking shrubs and planted new five- and six-foot pine trees.
- We hung planter boxes from the second level with

various hanging plants to enhance the looks of the place.

- Before undertaking any changes, we asked the few remaining tenants to leave, which they did without incident or court battles.
- A large, very nice looking sign made out of brick and cedar was placed at the entrance of the building with the new name of the building prominently displayed.
- We replaced all the broken windows and the kicked-in doors.
- We painted and recarpeted each unit.
- We resodded the lawns that came even close to needing it.
- We put up decorative, inexpensive wood numbers (bought at a close-out sale for next to nothing) on the side of the building to identify each apartment unit and took down the cheap-looking metal numbers that were on the door.
- We made sure that every single piece of paper and everything that might make the property at all tacky was picked up daily.

My overriding philosophy as I began this turnaround project was that you never get a second chance to make a first impression. This is true with property or a business. You can have the nicest interiors in town, but if your property doesn't seem special on the outside it will be very hard to get anyone to take the time to get behind the exterior. When beginning a turnaround project, I always start on the outside and then work in (most people do it the other way around).

HOW TO FILL UP A BUILDING FAST

Having fixed up the exterior, I started with an empty building. Not a single tenant means no income. I decided I would do everything possible to have some source of income during the several months of renovation. Knowing most people would not want to move in during a big mess, I decided to drop the rent drastically so I would have a line of people wanting to get in. I then sent a letter to the leaders of the many churches in the city outlining the strict qualifications and mentioning the low rent. I knew I had to screen very well because of the area and the security problems of the past.

From that mailout over five hundred persons applied for the one hundred units that were available. Subsequently, each tenant who moved in was told that rent would be at the reduced rate only for the first five months. Thereafter, it would go up in steps until it got to the market rate. I knew that by gradually moving the rent up later we would lose some tenants, but certainly not all, and it would give me time to fill the other units.

One year and three months later, after an expenditure of approximately $200,000, or $2000 a unit, the building was worth over a million dollars in excess of its worth when the project was started. (That's a five-to-one return on an investment— 500%.)

BRAVE VISION

Don't let the numbers scare you off. The same thing could have happened with a $2000 investment on a very small property with a $10,000 return.

For example, the Swiss Chalet was sold shortly after the renovations, which couldn't have cost more than $1000, were made. I don't know what the property sold for, but I do know that I suddenly wanted to buy it and that in my mind it was worth $10,000 more than when I had seen it previously.

In cases like that of the little house, once you have done exterior renovation it is easy to sell a prospective buyer on the dream of what could be done with the rest of the property, even if the inside hasn't been touched. It's fun, and usually very effective, to challenge the would-be buyer to be creative. Use statements like, "I know that most people aren't very creative and don't have the vision to see what can be done with this little place. I know I'm not very good at it, but maybe you can see great possibilities for this dumpy property."

SOME MBAS WON'T DIRTY THEIR HANDS

Remember Tai Vu? Through his hard work and that of his employees, his company is able to do janitorial work at $50 to $100 less than competing firms. Why? Because his employees, many of whom are family and friends, work for $4 an hour. Heavens, I know some fifteen- and sixteen-year-old kids who would be offended if you offered them a measly $4. They think that it's beneath them. Oh, do they have a lesson to learn. I also know college students with bachelors degrees or MBAs who think starting or running a janitorial service company is beneath them. They wouldn't dirty their hands on such menial tasks. Which is why they never will do more than work for someone else.

This is also one reason why many people in the business of buying yuk properties do not have college backgrounds. Many college grads just don't want to do all those "less-than-status" things that are required on the yuk properties to increase their value drastically. Consequently they miss out on some phenomenal financial opportunities.

FIX A TOILET: MAKE A FORTUNE

I remember when I graduated from college, I wanted the status of a white-collar job complete with a three-piece pin-stripe suit.

And that's exactly what I had until I realized that the big bucks aren't always in white-collar places. Sometimes I had to get down and do some less-than-status work to take advantage of the current opportunities. I mean, let's face it: fixing a broken toilet is no fun, nor is there any status in it. But fix the right toilet and there's a fortune in it for you. *Never let formal education make you think you are above certain kinds of work.* This takes courage, too.

LOTS OF HARD WORK AND COORDINATION

Table 1 shows you how you can accumulate $384,405 net in just two years. With only $3000 of your own cash and $2000 borrowed to begin with, you buy your first yuk property, using the $3000 for cash down and the $2000 borrowed money to refurbish. By making improvements that dramatically improve value, you move the value from $30,000 to $40,000. After sales commissions and closing costs, you net $10,000 on a $5000 investment, and this is done within three months.

Assuming you already know how to find property like this (see Chapter 6), and negotiate a good price to buy it (see Chapter 8), the one big remaining question is, how do you know what it is going to be worth when you finish fixing it up?

The value of anything is tricky and elusive. *The fair market*

Table 1

$384,405 NET IN TWO YEARS

	Your Cash	Borrowed Cash	Down Payment	Total Price	Fix-up Cost	New Improved Value	Net Sales After Costs		Total Profit
3 mos. 1st Property	$3000	$2000	$3000	$30,000	$2000	$40,000	$37,000	SP*	$37,000
								Mtg.	27,000
								PRO.	$10,000 on $5000 inv.
3 mos. 2nd Property	$10,000 ($2000 of which is borrowed)	$10,000	$10,000	$90,000	$10,000	$130,000	$120,000	SP	$120,000
								Mtg.	80,000
								PRO.	$40,000
6 mos. 3rd Property	$40,000	$40,000	$40,000	$375,000	$40,000	$525,000	$500,000**	SP	$500,000
								Mtg.	335,000
								PRO.	$165,000
12 mos. 4th Property	$165,000	$100,000	$100,000	$1,100,000	$115,000	$1,580,000	$1,510,000	SP	$1,510,000
								Mtg.	950,00
								PRO.	$560,000

Summary of Totals

Total Profit	$560,000
Less Borrowed funds	152,000
	$408,000
Less Accumulated Int.	23,595
Total Net Profit	$384,405

Interest Costs at Ave. of 13%

24 mos.	$2000	$520
21 mos.	10,000	2275
18 mos.	40,000	7800
12 mos.	100,000	13,000
		$23,595

Borrowed cash is from several banks on a short-term basis, preferably on signature loans at 1% or 2% over prime. These can be virtually perpetual by paying them off from new loans from different banks, alternating banks.

*SP = selling price

**Your cost of sales commission and closing costs normally drop as of percentage of total value with larger properties.

NOTE: I have assumed that all four properties would rent for enough to make the mortgage payment during renovations.

93

value of anything is whatever someone is willing to pay for it or sell it for at a given time. It does take some thought and energy to figure out what the maximum price you can sell a property for would be, and what specifically you need to do to get it there.

SWIMMING POOL, FLOWERBEDS, OR PICKET FENCE

If you buy a house and renovate it, making it a much nicer looking place as well as a nicer place in which to live, and your objective is to sell it to an owner/user, the criteria for its value should be set primarily by comparable properties in the neighborhood. If you added just the one extra-special feature to your property to make it much more desirable than the others around, whether it is a hot tub or swimming pool, flowerbeds in the front yard, a picket fence, or fancy kitchen cupboards, then possibly you could sell it for several thousand dollars more than the property next door. If, on the other hand, your property is to be sold to an investor who will not occupy it, then the primary value will be derived from income.

INCOME STREAM WILL TELL YOU WHAT TO DO

Income properties are bought, sold, and evaluated basically on income stream—the income generated from the property. Increase the income stream and you increase the value of the property. If you increase the income stream by 10% or 20%, you increase the value of the property by the same amount. Let's say the first property you bought rented for $300 before your renovations and after renovations it rented for $400. You have increased the rents 33% and hence the value of the property 33%. So the value of the building itself would also increase by 33% or more—from $30,000 to $40,000. As you contemplate what you want to fix, improve, and renovate in subsequent properties, be sure you do things that will allow you to increase the rental income by the percentage target that you have.

$40,000 PROFIT IN SIX MONTHS

In the second step of your two-year road to more than a third of a million dollars, you buy a $90,000 property with $10,000 down, using $10,000 borrowed money to renovate the property to increase its value to $130,000. After sales, commissions, and costs you now have accumulated a $40,000 profit, $12,000 of which is borrowed. Adding that to another $40,000 borrowed money, you buy the third property, putting the additional $40,000 of borrowed money into renovation and thus increasing the value to $525,000, or $500,000 net after cost.

The last step, which takes twelve months, is with your $165,000 cash you now have, $52,000 of which is borrowed. You add $100,000 borrowed money to buy a $1.1 million building. Using the $115,000 fix-up money wisely in places that will allow you to increase the rent by making the building a much nicer place to live, you increase the total value of the building to $1,510,000 net.

You end up with $560,000 net equity after paying off the $152,000 in loans. You end up with $408,000, and, after paying off the $23,595 in interest, you end up with a net profit of $384,405. And you have completed your task.

NO SECOND CHANCE TO MAKE A FIRST IMPRESSION

Before beginning on any one of the four properties, remember to take time to think. Think about the changes you are going to bring about. Think about your potential renter. From the street, what does he see first as he drives up to your building? Remember, you don't get a second chance to make a first impression. Do you need to take some trees down or to plant some? Do you need to cover the brick with wood? Or do you need to cover the wood with brick? Should you put some walls up or take some down? Does the driveway need to be redone? How about shrubs and sod, signs and lights, windows, doors? I have seen buildings where nothing other than putting a nice decorative door has totally changed the looks of the property. In fact, the whole focal point became the door, with a very nice aesthetic effect. Get help and ideas from friends and professionals.

Follow the four simple steps that I use before buying a yuk property:

STEP 1: Study and analyze the property, usually for at least an hour. If you force yourself to sit and look at something for an hour, it is amazing how many ideas you can come up with. Always have your yellow pad and pen handy to write down things that come to your mind. After analyzing and studying for an hour, take pictures. Then drive by other properties and take pictures of them, comparing the properties that have already been fixed up that are similar to the property you're thinking of buying. In addition, page through various house/gardening and apartment magazines for ideas on what can be done with the property. If you're like me and don't know what to do with the outside, have a professional architect or artist do a sketch or two of the exterior of the building suggesting inexpensive changes you could make that would have a dramatic effect for the eye appeal of the building. Drive through the neighborhood so you get to know it well. It takes only a few minutes to get a general feeling for the area. Take time to check rents in the buildings that are nearby and similar. All you have to do is walk up to them and pose as a prospective tenant and you will quickly see what the going rents in the area are.

PROJECT YOUR PROFIT BEFORE YOU BUY

STEP 2: Do a cost estimate of the changes you think will be necessary to make the yuk property into a very desirable property. If needed, I get bids or estimates from contractors or subcontractors. Many times, the work that needs to be done can be done by semiskilled hourly help, or if you want free help, ask the wife, kids, relatives, friends. Within Step 2 always make an estimate of the new value after the projected renovations are completed. Then decide if the reward is worth the effort and the risk.

If, for example, I plan to put $5000 into a property and my estimated reward will be an increased value of, let's say, $7000, for a new profit of $2000, then I would not go ahead because the reward is not worth the effort and the risk. If, on the other hand, that $5000 estimate were going to net at least $10,000, it would seem well worth the effort and the risk. (Although this is an individual value judgment, I strongly advise that you leave room for error. There are very few of us who don't make mistakes once in a while.)

STEP 3: Make an offer based on Step 2, an offer that will assure you a wide enough estimated margin. I usually make my first offer low enough that I can raise it and still hit my target.

STEP 4: After closing, begin renovations. Set up a time schedule for each step of the renovation, with deadlines on each phase.

This is critical because without deadlines you will inevitably stretch the work over a much longer period of time than you had planned. This is very expensive—a budget breaker. If you have people doing the work for you, be sure that you place the responsibility of the deadline on them and tell them that the work has to be done by that deadline. If they are subcontractors, you must get more than an oral agreement that the job will be done by a certain date. With only an oral agreement, you will find that the job stretches for weeks and months beyond deadlines. You will get a lot of excuses, but it won't get done on time and you will lose money from their negligence.

A $200-A-DAY PENALTY WILL WORK MIRACLES

Not too long ago I put in a swimming pool and a tennis court at the back of my property. It had to be finished by August 19 at the very latest because of a very important party I had arranged. I called various contractors, shopping for the best price, and asked them if they could meet my deadline. All of them asssured me that they could do it, even though it would be really pushing it. I told them that I wanted a clause in the contract providing a $200-a-day penalty if the jobs were not done by August 19. Suddenly I started getting excuses from most of the bidders. When they saw that I insisted on having a finish date in writing, complete with a penalty clause, most dropped out, saying they knew they could do it by then, but would not agree to the penalty. The salty old Norwegian swimming-pool contractor who took the contract completed the pool in thirteen days, a week before the deadline. He began digging two hours after signing.

The tennis-court contractor made the deadline too, though his men were painting the last lines on the court as the party guests arrived.

If you want a job done on time, get it in writing and make sure you have a penalty clause. You will be glad you did. Remember, money is relative only to one thing: time. If I say that I made $50,000, that really doesn't tell you anything until I tell you how long it took me to make it. If it took me ten years, I didn't do so well. If I did it in ten days, that's phenomenal.

You and I not only need to set deadlines with accompanying penalties when dealing with employees, associates, and contractors but with ourselves too. We need to set tough deadlines for ourselves and use discipline if we expect to rise above the average. Lock yourself into some deadline that you can't get out of and you'll amaze yourself by what you can accomplish.

DON'T LET THE DETAILS SLOW YOU DOWN

The mechanics of buying property slow many people down. They get all excited and want to get started but they don't know exactly what to do. The good news is that the mechanics are fairly simple to learn. For many years my financial progress was retarded because I didn't understand the mechanics of buying a property. I didn't know which papers or forms or contracts to use. I didn't know how to write a contract and was fearful of asking anyone to show me exactly how. Fortunately, I was taken under the wing of an older realtor who shared his experience and practical knowledge with me.

There is one key document that you should get to know thoroughly, which will help you get going and overcome any reluctance you might have. That document is called an earnest-money offer. It is the document that accompanies your earnest-money check. It has different names in different states, but by and large it contains the same basic clauses. It is the first written document that one uses in making an offer on a property. Any realtor has copies of it and would be glad to give you one. You can also buy the pre-printed form at legal stationery stores. Read the document and reread it. You will quickly see that most of it is boilerplate legal language. There are blanks to be filled in with the description of the property, its price, the terms you are offering, and other identifying characteristics and specific clauses you wish to insert.

What you must understand is that this form can be changed. It can be customized to fit your own needs—within limits, of course. You can't modify clauses that are state statutes, but there are very few of these. The blanks to be filled in are the keys to your success or failure. Clauses such as the "weasel," or "escape," clause, or the "subject-to" clause prevent you from losing your earnest-money offer by giving you an out if you can't complete the deal. You can also make many offers, as detailed in Chapter 6.

Be sure that you use these blanks to tell the other party exactly what you want and what you will accept. Be specific in your language, using all necessary details so that there is no misunderstanding. On the first few offers that you make, it would be wise to have an attorney, real-estate broker or agent, or someone who has used the form many times before help you. Look over what you have written to make sure you haven't made any mistakes that will get you into trouble. You want your yuks to make big bucks.

8

NINE NEGOTIATING HINTS FOR HIGH RETURN ON INVESTMENTS

Make a 100% return on your money (starting with $1000) for just ten years and you'll be a millionaire. That's easy to say, and mathematically sound, but how do you make a 100%? It's really quite simple. You can wait for inflation to do the job (see Chapter 4), or you can create the inflation yourself by fixing up yuks. But there's another way, which may be the cleanest way of all—by negotiating.

Assume, for example, you are able to buy an asset for 5% less than its real market value because of your negotiating skills, then, within a year, you are able to negotiate a sale for 5% above the fair market value. The bottom line of those negotiations is that you made yourself a full 100% return on your investment by negotiating well. *The key is skillful negotiations, and the skillfulness is developed through study, practice, and effort.*

JAW, JAW ALONE CAN MAKE YOU 150%

Winston Churchill said, "Jaw, Jaw is better than War, War!" And I say that jaw, jaw can make you rich, rich. If you use the right negotiating words and actions, you can make a 150% return on your investment just from your talk (See Example 2, Table 1).

When I made an offer on a large student-housing complex, I knew I was making a very low offer. When the seller started shuttling my negotiator back and forth in his corporate jet, I was certain that the seller was motivated. By long and careful negotiations (Jaw, Jaw), I finally ended up buying the building for $500,000 less than the current market value.

Negotiating is both a science and an art. It can be subtle or blunt. Sometimes you should use a hardheaded frontal attack and other times you need to take your time and stroke the seller or buyer. If you are good, (and a good part of being good is learned), you can make yourself wealthy using just your mind and your mouth.

BRAIN IN GEAR BEFORE ENGAGING MOUTH

Before the tongue starts to wag, the brain needs to work and work hard. You must be a very aware person and plan your strategy carefully. You need to be aware of what the other party wants. To persuade people, show them the value of what you are selling in terms of meeting their needs and desires. *Successful negotiation comes from figuring out what the other person wants and showing him or her a way to get it.* You get what you want, too.

HIDDEN AGENDAS

The problem is that most people won't tell you what they want. Don't get me wrong. They think they are telling you what they want, and a lot of words will come out of their mouth, but most of the time they don't know what they want. The typical seller or buyer throws up a smokescreen without even knowing he is doing it. Therefore, you must develop an awareness not only to what he is saying but, more important, to what he is not saying. You must read between the lines and be aware of a person's entire situation. You must guess the hidden agenda.

By careful observation and the right kind of questions, a good negotiator knows within minutes what method will be most effective for negotiating the best possible deal.

AN ALERT BROKER—AN UNFORGETTABLE LESSON

When I was training to be a stockbroker, I spent a day with an institutional broker who was a master negotiator. While walking out of the bank after meeting with a bank trust officer for thirty or forty minutes, this seasoned broker turned to me and said, "It's very helpful to now know that they are buying stock through Merrill Lynch and E. F. Hutton and also to know that they just bought 50,000 shares of General Electric. And it's too bad that he is being audited personally by the IRS. By the way, did you notice that he is a real tennis nut? And I'm pretty sure he has major problems with his wife right now."

I looked at him in total disbelief and said, "How in the world do you know all that? I didn't hear him say one word about any of those things."

He proceeded to give me a lesson on awareness—one I have never forgotten. While we were sitting there, his eyes were scanning the bank officer's entire office, including his desk top, on which rested stacks of papers that were topped by confirmation slips of the 50,000 shares of General Electric that he had bought. Also on the desk was correspondence from the brokerage firms of Merrill Lynch and E. F. Hutton. I had not even seen the small tennis trophy on the credenza behind the broker. My friend, whose eyes and mind were alert, had picked up the marital problems from the man's facial expression when he asked how his kids were doing.

THE MIND IS QUICKER THAN THE TONGUE

By keeping your mind very alert and questioning yourself throughout a conversation, you can learn five times more than someone who is not actively trying to be aware. Remember that the mind can think much faster than you can talk. This gives you time to listen to what the person is saying and to formulate many questions about what you should look for, observe, and be aware of.

NINE NEGOTIATING HINTS

The following nine negotiating hints have been proven to work on thousand-dollar deals and multimillion-dollar deals alike. Try them and you'll see for yourself. Remember: saving just 5% on each end of a deal can make you 100% on your money!

1. LABOR UNIONS MAKE A TON OF DOUGH WITH THIS ONE: THE LIST TECHNIQUE

People who want to do things fast, the efficient people, use lists. These lists are prioritized. Being clear about your priorities is essential in negotiating skillfully.

It works for kids. Your junior-high daughter asks if she can sleep over at her friend's house and you say, "No."

"Well, how about if my friend sleeps over here?"

Your answer is still no.

"Can I then at least go out shopping with her tonight? We'll be back early."

No.

"Can she at least come over and watch TV? There's a good movie on and it'll be over by eleven o'clock."

"Well" (pause), "okay," you reluctantly respond.

Bingo, she has won: score, daughter 1, father 0. She had a list for you, and by design or by just feminine intuition from her list of four, she got you to give in on possibly the only item she really wanted. The first three were just a smokescreen to make it seem that she was giving in on the bulk of requests. Number four was the true objective in the first place.

1. Sleep at friend's house
2. Friend sleeps at her house
3. Go shopping at the mall
4. Watch movie till eleven P.M.

Your daughter would possibly have liked items one, two, or three, but she probably knew there was no way you would give in, so perhaps she wasn't planning on them. But she surrendered on each of the first three, building you up for the kill, number four. If you had given her a negative response on number four, she would have had lots of ammo to shoot you down.

"Dad, give me a break—you won't let me sleep at Cindy's house or let her sleep here and we can't even go to the mall for a few minutes. So at least let us watch the movie tonight. She'll go home right after the movies. Dad, really—let us have at least a little fun!"

What a setup. It is quite obvious what's happening when you think of it in its entirety. But it works every single day and in every single city and in every single home.

Copy Kids and Unions

Maybe kids don't consciously plan out this kind of strategy beforehand, but you better believe the subconscious is working overtime so they can reach their objective. And we as adults should get our minds working the same way on our deals.

The use of lists when dealing with business propositions, or when buying an income property or any business asset, really does work because people respond to what seems to be fair. Sometimes you need to point out to the other party all of the concessions you are making on your long list of demands.

Unions in America have been using the list technique for years, and have been negotiating the socks off otherwise astute corporations. They offer management a long list of items that they say they need. Most of the items won't be critical ones. On these they will make many concessions, building up credits, establishing themselves as friendly and flexible. But toward the end of the list lies their real objective, and it is usually money. They will concede on how many tables should be in the coffee-break room, but they will hold firm on the $2.50 hourly wage increase.

First Item on the List: Make a List

Let's say you are trying to buy an appreciating asset. The first thing you should do is to sit down and make a list of your objectives, demands, and things you would like to have. Put the items that are most important to you toward the end of the list and the least-important items (ones that are, however, important to some people) toward the beginning. For example:

1. The price you want.
2. The roof to be repaired by the seller before closing.
3. A new carpet to be installed in the back rooms by the seller.
4. The dilapidated building in the back of the property to be torn down.
5. The date you want possession of the asset.
6. How much cash you are willing to put down (if you are buying).
7. What interest rate you will pay or receive.

On the above list, the price appears first because in buying most assets it is not usually a critical item (as you will see from Chapter 10). But the amount of cash down and the interest rate paid or received can be very critical, so negotiate hardest on these items. If, however, you are paying all cash for an asset, then price would probably be put toward the end of the list because it would be more important, possibly your key negotiating objective.

Carefully Compromise

Assume this is not a cash transaction and that the seller is willing to carry some of the financing (whether it is an income property or a business or some other kind of appreciating asset). After terminating negotiations on the possession date, you should gradually concede on other initial demands until you get your cash down, or the desired interest rate: things that are essential to your profiting on the deal. It is in negotiating these later points that your earlier concessions can be used to get your terms. (I point out that I have compromised on the other items—one, two, three, four, and so on, whatever they are—so in fairness if the other party really wants to sell (or buy, whichever the case may be) he or she surely needs to do a little compromising too, and should meet me halfway.) And this, of course, is what I specifically point out to him.

Practice this skill. Learn to compromise on the unessential in order to give clout to your firmness on downpayment and interest rates, which are critical for profit. You can add to your list as many possible points to be considered for compromise as you need to show yourself reasonable in the negotiating process, just as the unions do.

Union Demand Lists: A Pattern

Remember the typical union demand lists and how they load the top of them with washroom and coffee-break items and leave the request for a $2.50 raise at the bottom. It works for them, it works for the wealthy, who have been doing it for years, and it will work for you. So do it next time you buy an appreciating asset you want. Take the time to make a good-sized demand list. Take the time to study it and have enough verbal ammo to discuss each item. Don't compromise and surrender the top items on the list too fast or it will be obvious that they really don't matter to you.

Parade Your Particular Concessions

Lastly, be sure to point out each of your compromises, making sure the seller or buyer sees that you are trying to satisfy both his needs and yours. Say to him, "Look, I'm trying to make this deal work. Sure I'm looking out for myself, but I've given or compromised on some of these items. If you want to sell (or buy), then you have to do the same and meet me halfway."

2. WIN-WIN

"If you can show me how to win and how to win big, I will give you just about anything you want." Isn't this the key to most of our negotiating today? Isn't this what a good salesman does when he or she tries to sell you something? He tries to show you that what you are buying can help you just as much as the sale will help him. I'm sure that you would pay me a hundred thousand dollars tomorrow if I could show you how to make two hundred thousand that same day. That is the essence of win-win in negotiating.

Insane Deal Creates Two Winners

Darreld Martin must not read the papers. Doesn't he know that there is no money available for investments? Doesn't he know that there aren't any deals out there anymore? Besides, if he wins on this deal, won't that make John Hagman, the seller, a loser?

Here's the story. Mr. John Hagman had a nice apartment building in a good location, with excellent tenants, and he had a respectable cash flow. But John had just retired and decided to cash in on his investment. He wanted to travel and see the world.

So he put the property up for sale, and bingo, to John's delight it sold and sold fast. The buyer of John's property is convinced that John has lost all his marbles, but is he ever glad!

The buyer, Darreld Martin, knows that John is not permanently insane, but that he was a motivated seller. It was an *insane deal* for sure, but nobody was really crazy because both parties came out the winner.

Creative Financing

The real key to this great transaction was a bit of creative financing. That creative financing allowed Mr. Martin to buy Mr. Hagman's property without a single cent of his own cash. And when the deal closed, Darreld Martin (remember, he is the buyer) actually put *several thousand dollars' cash* in his pocket.

That's what creative financing is all about. Most people don't understand such crazy deals, but they are really quite simple—you just need to follow the right steps.

How was Hagman able to come out so well, too? He agreed

to "subordinate his interest," thus allowing Martin to put a new first mortgage on the property (this gave the seller cash, with Hagman carrying a low-interest second mortgage, and allowed the buyer to get some cash from the first mortgage, too. Pretty slick). When all the dust settled, both Martin and Hagman had cash in their pockets.

Hagman is now enjoying his cash in Europe and Martin is ready to buy another property with his.

Does Someone Have to Lose?

Most people are convinced that when one person profits from a deal another person automatically has to lose. This is not true. Business deals are not sports. There need not always be a winner and a loser. Business is contribution and productivity. It's the process of providing goods and services to people. It's helping people. It's fulfilling needs. And if you can figure out what people really want, or what they think they want, our economy will reward you in proportion to your contribution.

Figure Others' Wants

The trouble is that most people don't stop to figure out what others want. They just start talking or arguing, mistakenly thinking that is negotiating. It is said of Napoleon that he won his battles in his tent before ever taking the field. A good negotiator does the same thing. He thinks through the entire negotiating process before he begins negotiating. As he thinks, he writes down those things that will help him.

If you are smart, you will think through the negotiating process beforehand. You will put on your list an item that will help the other party win. You want to tell him that, right up front, so you'll put it at the top of the list. What does the other person need? What does he want? I mean, what does he *really* want and need? You show him how he can win, especially in the first or second step, and you will both win.

Turn Out the Lights But Don't Go to Sleep

A sixty-two-year-old New York man wants to sell his business (or an apartment building). He wants all cash because he has worked hard and finally wants to enjoy the fruits of his efforts. He is asking $175,000 for his appreciating assets, which he has owned for seventeen years. The asset is now free and clear of any mortgage or bank loan.

You want the asset. It is a good one and meets all your needs. But for the $175,000 cash he wants, no way. Even if you had that kind of cash, you wouldn't put it all on this one deal. And the fact is, you don't happen to have $175,000 lying around. So what do you do about it? Try turning out the lights, but don't go to sleep. It's time to think.

Think about the seller and get to know him in your mind. He's worked hard. He's done well and wants to take it easy now. That's reasonable. How can you help him reach his goals and turn the deal into a win-win situation?

The first question that you will probably want to ask is, What is he going to do with the cash that he will receive? The second question: Does he really need all of the $175,000 right now? Why not find out by talking directly to him or through a middle-man, broker, or agent? Let's say you find out that he has planned a worldwide one-year trip, then he plans to retire in Phoenix. In a year, after the trip, he'll have the cost of moving from New York to Phoenix, where in the warmth of the Arizona sun he will live off the interest from the balance of the $175,-000.

Therefore He Doesn't Need All Cash

Through reason and research you have discovered that he really doesn't need all that cash up front. Now it is fairly easy to structure a win-win deal by giving the seller enough cash down to cover his two big expenses: First, his world trip and second, his move from New York to Phoenix. Then the balance of what you owe him can be paid over a number of years, so that he has enough to live on and so that the monthly payments you need to make can be covered by the income you'll receive from his own asset that you bought. You could even offer to find several condos in the Phoenix area from which he could pick during his one-year trip. On his arrival, all he would have to do is fly to Phoenix and be chauffeured around by you to see the properties that you tied up for him by the wise use of the "subject-to" clause.

You have solved three big problems for the seller. Number 1, he sells what he wants and he does it now; Number 2, he gets the cash he needs plus income to live on later; and, Number 3, you have helped him and given him red-carpet service (which we all love) by doing a lot of his legwork in a new town to find a place where he can live. Best of all, by doing this you probably will get exactly what you want. It could turn out to be a real win-win situation—two winners and no losers. Ten or fifteen years from now you may sell it exactly as he did to someone exactly like you for another win-win negotiated deal.

3. NEGOTIATIONS—LOGIC MIXED WITH PRE-THINKING

Thinking pays big, but pre-thinking pays bigger. The trouble with thinking is that it's hard—most people would rather take it easy. But if you do the thinking *before* you negotiate, you won't be trapped when someone asks you a tough question. You will have a good answer because you have pre-thought the conversation. You will have thought through the situation and know all the questions and answers before they ever come up. In fact, if you spend enough time thinking ahead before your negotiating sessions, you'll end up asking most of the questions during the sessions, which will give you the upper hand.

I've seen people get trapped at the closing table because they were not prepared. I saw a seller put in a penalty clause for late payment right on the spot, even though the parties hadn't previously agreed to such a clause. The fellow merely asked the buyer if he was going to be on time with all his payments.

The buyer said, "Yes, of course."

"Then," replied the seller, "I am sure you won't mind my putting this penalty clause in here for any late payments."

"Ahh-hhh," said the buyer, "I suppose not."

The buyer was not at all pleased with the deal, but he was trapped because he hadn't pre-thought the situation. He lacked the right words to counter the seller's query. He lacked confidence to make a stand because of the temporary confusion in his mind as to just exactly what to say. So he took the easy course. He created no waves. He said to himself, "Well, it's no big deal anyway and I probably won't ever be late."

As a matter of fact, it could be a very big deal. If the buyer had thought it out in advance, he never would have been trapped. In a crunch he should have had a few standard "buy-some-time" phrases in mind to throw out to stop the flow of events for a while. Keep in mind phrases such as the following, to be used for "stall time." While you are at it, take time to develop your own standard phrases for awkward situations.

- "Wait a minute—let's discuss (or talk about, or think about, or explore) that comment." Then quickly go through his or her proposal in your mind and ask questions. Questioning is not only a great way to buy time, it is also an excellent and effective negotiating technique because it puts the other person on the defensive. But don't overuse it or be too demanding. Don't make the other person feel as though he were on the witness stand.

- A catch-all question the buyer can throw back at the seller is, "Now let me think—was that clause something that we agreed to in our preliminary agreement?" Then reach for the agreement and start looking for the clause (which of course you know isn't there). As you look, you have time to think of something to say that is polite and yet shows that you are taking a firm stand against the addition of this or any other clause that might come up. After looking for a few minutes, you say, "No, it's not here. We didn't agree to that, so it wouldn't be fair to put it in right now. Don't worry, I won't be late with my payments in any case."

- "I'll need time to run that idea (or question or new part of the contract or deal) past my partner (attorney, CPA, financial adviser, wife, girlfriend, or banker)."

- "I really don't have time to discuss (or talk about or think about) it right now. Let's meet tomorrow at my office."

- "I'm not sure I understand what you're saying. Back up and start over."

To win at negotiating you need logic on your side. Logic is expressed by words, and without the proper words in your mind, you will lose, so be prepared. Refer to the key phrases above and be familiar with them. Have them ready in your mind so you can win at negotiating through pre-thinking and logic.

4. TANGIER RUG LESSON

Not long ago I sponsored a special investors' seminar in Spain, and while there we took the hydrofoil across the Straits of Gibraltar to Africa and toured the city of Tangier.

The tour was arranged ahead of time, and the talkative guides took us through the narrow, winding back streets, through the open markets with their pungent odors. Then, after half an hour's stop at the Casbah, we finally ended up at a rug merchant's large second-floor shop.

It was there in the next hour or so that some shrewd negotiating took place. We were hot and tired, sitting comfortably on mounds of beautiful Oriental rugs. Our gracious host began telling the group about the uniqueness of his rugs. Then his troupe of articulate salespeople proceeded to sell their captive audience on the quality of the merchandise. They explained the custom of haggling over price. They would be offended if we were to accept their first price without some sporty bargaining. The price on one rug was $4500. Priming the crowd in a jovial joking mood, the merchant asked for someone to make him an offer. He wanted an offer, no matter how ridiculous. Well, someone in the crowd humored him with an offer of $500. And from that point the haggling, or negotiating, started in earnest. After a few minutes I couldn't even hear what was going on because the salespeople had divided the group into smaller groups and were noisily haggling away.

I found out later that the $4500 rug had gone for $1200. The buyer had been assured that its value was over $2000. He received the written appraisal stating that fact. A couple of months later he had the rug appraised in the States and found out that its true market value was $600.

The Oldest Gimmick in the Book

It's one of the oldest gimmicks in the book—starting with a very high price to give the illusion of a bargain when the price is cut dramatically. Thousands of stores use this technique every single day of the year. And you know what? It keeps working and working. We all love to buy something on sale. If we see on the ticket that it has been marked down from $180 to $99, we feel that we are getting a terrific deal. A lot can be learned from this if you just think about it for a while. *Whether you are buying or selling, start the bargaining process with a price substantially different from your target price.*

When I bought the student-housing complex mentioned earlier, the seller was asking $3.4 million for it. Although he was willing to carry the financing, he wanted 11% interest. My target price was $2.5 million with 7% financing, so my beginning offers on the property were $2.1 million on the price and a ridiculously low 4%. By starting much lower than the two targets I had for interest rate and price, I was able to give and take and finally ended up on target.

If you are selling an asset, price it high enough so you can reduce your price substantially to give the illusion that it's a real bargain for the buyer.

This is elementary, but it is so elementary that many people today don't think that this technique will work when selling investment items. Consequently they miss out on maximizing their profits. They are too proud to haggle!

5. BONUS FROM BLUFFING

Some years ago I walked into an Audi dealership to look at their cars. I wanted to buy a new car and saw a beautiful red Audi LS 100. After checking it out thoroughly, I sat down with the salesman and a friend of mine who had come along to shop with me. I started the negotiating process by making a ridiculously low offer, to which the salesman made a counteroffer. I bumped my offer up a little bit and he came down a little bit. He finally came down to where we were just a few hundred dollars apart, and finally he announced that this was as low as he could go, whereupon I announced that my price was as high as I could go.

I was bluffing, but he didn't know that. He was bluffing also, only I didn't know that for sure. But he had more to lose than I did, so my friend and I got up, thanked him for his time, and told him how sorry I was I couldn't get the car, because I really wanted it, but that I had given him my top price. As we walked toward the door I said to my friend, "Don't look back! Just keep walking and see if he does anything." Well, we got to the door and nothing happened. We stepped outside and the door closed behind us. I turned to my friend and said, "Well, I guess we lost! I really thought he'd stop us."

I was just about ready to turn around and go back, because I had decided I was going to buy the car. You see, I knew I could walk out of the showroom just to see if he would stop me. If he didn't, I could always go back in and tell him I had changed my mind. I could then pay the full price that he was asking. Before I had a chance to turn around, I heard the door open and the voice of the salesman saying, "Wait a minute! Listen, you guys, it's past closing time and I haven't had a sale today. Let's go ahead and write it up. I'll agree to your price." I went ahead and bought the car, and saved over $300. This is not a lot of money, but it does make the point. Besides, my effort to save that $300 was minimal.

Heads I Win, Tails I Win

People bluff at poker all the time. The problem is that in poker, if you bluff and someone calls your bluff, you lose. In negotiating to buy or sell appreciating assets, there is a big bonus. If you bluff and win, you win. If you bluff and lose, you still can win. If the car salesman had called my bluff and hadn't called me back, I still wouldn't have lost anything because I still would have ended up buying what I wanted to buy.

The key to bluffing is that you absolutely cannot show one single, solitary crack or let it be known that you are bluffing. Like a good actor, you have to play the part to the hilt, not falling out of character even for a moment.

I Even Fooled My Comptroller

Some time ago I needed to borrow $100,000 to renovate a project I was working on. So I asked my comptroller to apply for a $100,000 loan at one percentage point over prime rate. He returned to the office the next day and told me he had met with the bank, and the bank was willing to lend the money but they insisted on my signing personally rather than just as a corporate officer. I told my comptroller that there was no way I would sign my name personally. We had dealt with the bank long enough that they should accept my signature as a corporate officer only. There was no need for me to obligate myself personally. My comptroller was quite put out with me. He said, "Mark, you know that we need the money." But even at that point I resisted telling him that I was bluffing.

He left the office convinced that the bank would not grant the loan unless I signed. He returned later with a surprised look on his face. "I can't believe they accepted the papers without your signing personally. I'm shocked." Only then did I tell him that I had been bluffing and that I would have signed if they had pushed it any further than they did.

Many times in the bluffing process you have to have a tremendous amount of patience. If you have bluffed before, your opponent will suspect that you are doing it again and will try to outbluff you by telling you he won't accept whatever you have offered. And he will want to wait a day or two to see if you change your mind. It is here that your patience is important. You need to outwait him. The younger, the more inexperienced a person is, the less patient he is.

Take for example the young man who goes to a used-car dealer to buy a car. He finds one that he falls in love with. Inevitably the salesman will tell him that someone was in earlier looking at the car, and, "if you want this car, young man, you'd better buy it now because he's coming back and will probably take it." Anybody who has gone looking for a used car has heard that line many times. Here you need to use patience. The car will wait. There is a 90% chance (or more) that the salesman is bluffing. If you don't believe me, go out and make a survey: when you hear that statement, wait a week, then go back to see if the same car is still there. The problem with many people is they fear losing what they think is the best deal of their life. First of all, it probably isn't the best deal of their life, and secondly, they probably won't even lose it.

The big bonus in bluffing comes when you make a ridiculously low offer on an asset—a total bluff—and to your surprise someone accepts it without any changes or compromises. You were bluffing but they didn't know it. Perhaps the person was a very highly motivated seller who grabbed the only offer. So you won and you won big. Granted, this doesn't happen every day, but if you are in the marketplace, making lots of offers, it will happen enough times to make people think you are a genius and call you lucky and enough times to make you wealthy.

6. WEAR THE SON-OF-A-GUN DOWN

Jake Ebach, who lives in the Midwest, needed a substantial loan for a project he was working on. Mr. Ebach presented his loan request to four different banks. Each bank turned him down. Not a man to give up easily, Jake tried again. But even the second approach met with the same response. Still determined to get the needed money, he approached each of the banks again. Finally, in round three, Jake scored a knockout.

Jake Ebach didn't keep going back with the same questions. Each time he went into a bank he was prepared with new proposals, new ways of meeting the objections they had for turning down prior requests. He was building a case and presenting it to the bank to prove that he wouldn't fail with his project. Let's face it. Any banker has to sit up and take notice when somebody is that persistent. I am sure the banker projected Jake's persistence into the project and reasoned that if he used that same persistence in making his project go, the possibility of failure was slim. Therefore he was a good loan risk.

As pointed out at the beginning of this chapter, there are many ways to negotiate. This is just one. The persistence approach. Asking over and over again. Showing the party with whom you are negotiating that you won't give up no matter what.

7. DIPLOMACY: BE MR. NICE GUY

Think for a minute who in the entire world is your best friend, the person you would do anything for. If you were very well off and had more money than you knew what to do with, and had an appreciating asset to sell cheap, and ten people wanted to buy it, how long would it take you to decide to sell it to your friend?

People say that it isn't what you know but who you know. The statement is partly true because most of us would rather do business with people we know, especially our good friends. Friends can be made quickly by diplomatic people, ones who know how to say the right thing at the right time, and who know when to keep their mouth shut if tempted to say the wrong thing.

I am not talking about flattery, which almost everyone can see right through. But a diplomatic, aware person can quickly identify those traits that are admirable in the person he is talking to. After recognizing what interests the other person, he or she then compliments or makes positive statements about those items. Honest statements about real traits enhance self-image and signal others that you are telling the truth.

The same technique must be applied when you are trying to buy an office building. It makes no sense to put the seller on the defensive by making comments about how poorly the building is being managed, a direct reflection on the owner. Even if the building has been beaten up badly and indicates poor management, a much more diplomatic way to say this would be something like, "You know, it's really a shame what some tenants do to beat up a building. Look what they've done with the copy machine; they just about destroyed the wall behind it." You have made your point and you haven't offended the seller.

Of course, what you say is only a part of diplomacy. What you do is critical. Doing special things can draw attention to you in a positive way. Years ago, I was trying to rent a million names from the American Express list and I needed the list in a hurry, faster than the normal procedure would get me the list. In desperation, I finally sent a dozen roses to one of the key women in their New York office. Well, this woman hadn't received very many roses, at least in the course of business, and so my gesture stood out and made a difference. The service that we received from that point on was phenomenal. I am sure that she hasn't forgotten it to this day, even though I haven't had contact with her for years.

All of us like people to pay attention to us, and the more sincere it is the more we like it. If you want to negotiate and win, be a real diplomat. Cater to the needs of the buyer or seller. Become their friend. Make yourself so valuable through word and deed that they will do almost anything for you. If they really like you, they are more apt to do business with you.

8. BUFFER ZONE

"You tell the seller that his price is so far out of line that it even fails to qualify as a joke. The guy must be nuts if he thinks I'm dumb enough not to see the problem he has. No wonder he wants to sell."

"Okay," says the agent. "I'm meeting with the seller this afternoon and I'll tell him."

When he meets the seller, the agent says, "Listen, I talked to the buyer this morning and he thinks we just may have a deal—a few changes will have to be made. He's a little concerned about some of the problems but I'm sure we can work something out."

The buyer was obviously quite emotional, but the agent took the emotion out of the buyer's words and no doubt moved the parties closer toward a deal. Had the agent quoted the buyer, the seller no doubt would have responded with similar words, thus killing any hopes of consummating a deal.

Using a middleman can do wonders for your wealth. Many people are always trying to save money, and I understand that, but the right middleman (or woman) can pay for himself many times over. He acts as a buffer zone to cushion abrasive words, actions, and emotions because he is in a position to be more objective.

True, he has a commission to earn, but many times without his skill and persistence, the deal wouldn't go through at all. That commission, which so many people begrudge him, motivates him to keep pushing the parties together. Oh, yes, there may be a lot of lazy, uninformed, and greedy agents who don't want to earn what they get, but *good* middlemen are worth their weight in gold.

- They supply education and information. All you have to do is ask, then listen.
- They supply excellent contacts with the right people at the right time.
- Commissioned agents don't lose you anything until the job is completely done.
- They save you a bundle of your precious time.
- They help you and the other party to overcome inertia.
- They keep tempers and emotions in proper perspective so the deal can continue toward a settlement.

I think middleman negotiating is great, but there are some do's and don'ts.

- Do use the best in town. Ask around (they're usually the busiest).
- Do, when possible, use one who specializes in whatever you're dealing in.
- Do use your own employees, friends, associates, rather than negotiating directly.
- Don't tell agents all that you're thinking (for example, what your highest price is).
- Don't accept the agent's word as to whether the deal is good or not good (remember, he or she stands to make money from it).

A good middleman can save a deal that might otherwise have been lost. So use these people and their skills.

9. INTIMIDATION/VICTIMIZATION

You walk into your office on Monday morning and find out you didn't get the raise you'd planned on for over a year. You are naturally upset; you feel like a victim. After all, you really deserved the raise. But now the tables start to turn as you avoid talking to your boss. When you can't avoid him any longer, you give him the silent treatment. You pout, you sulk, you act mad. Remember, you are fully justified. Now who is the victim? The boss is now feeling guilty. He probably knew you deserved the raise. Even if no one received a raise because of poor profits, he still feels the pressure. The silence is getting to him. You are intimidating him. You are controlling him by your actions. You are victimizing him by playing as if you were the victim.

This manipulation occurs daily in business, in politics, and in families (especially between husband and wife), and it works. Those who use it are dealing on a childish level. And when they get caught and the intimidation doesn't work, they have to dig deeper and try harder to act as if they were the victim.

Don't act the victim in business. You can win through intimidation—and many people do—but you may end up without any friends, or worse. To intimidate someone is literally to make him or her timid, and it does work, but it really doesn't show your courage. People do give in to the pressure that is put upon them. If you've ever been pushed into buying or selling against your will or judgment, then you know the negative feelings you harbored toward the offending party. If you want to use this method of negotiating, you should at least understand the price you may have to pay.

It is important however to recognize when someone is trying to intimidate you, because your early recognition of their attempt can totally thwart it. Thwarting intimidators builds up your courage.

Below is a list of things people say and do in an attempt to intimidate you:

- Give you the silent treatment, pout, cry, or sulk;
- Act put-out or mad ('cause you "done them wrong");
- Tell you they are losing money at the price they are buying or selling;
- Give you money or gifts to make you feel obligated;

- Do favors for you to make you feel obligated;
- Drop names: people, places, prestigious brand names, etc.

The last two items can be very effective intimidators, but if you use them, use them sparingly.

9

CASH COMING OUT OF YOUR YEARS

The longer you live, the more cash you should have. Yet there are millions of people who never seem to have any. You don't need to wait years before you have a lot of cash. There are ways and means of accumulating large amounts of it. Cash is critical. You've gotta have it. And lots of it. But it's really not that hard to get. It takes some discipline and a system, but with those two things you can always have large stashes of cash. Best of all, it really doesn't much matter what your income is right now. The important thing is to save some of it.

SIMULTANEOUS BORROWING AND SAVING

If you have saved $25,000 and it's just sitting there in your savings account in the bank, you are in a very good position when an ideal investment pops up. You are in the position to take advantage of it. You can buy it. You can do it right now. Not only that, with that $25,000 in the bank, the likelihood of an ideal investment popping up is much greater, since you most probably are already out looking for that investment. It is tough to save $25,000, everybody knows that, but through simultaneous borrowing and saving it can be done. I said earlier that it takes discipline to save, and it does, but you can force that discipline.

Instead of borrowing $10,000 or $15,000 to buy a car, which is certain to depreciate in value, why not stick that borrowed money in your savings account, at least temporarily?

Forty-eight months later, when you pay off the loan, you would still have $15,000 in the bank. And it will have grown to a larger amount because of the interest accrued. Sure, you also will have paid interest on the loan, probably a little larger amount than the interest you received. But the point is that you have forced yourself into a corner; you have forced yourself to save money.

Ralph Waldo Emerson said what he needed most was for someone to get him to do those things he already knew he should do. I've outlined above a system of simultaneously borrowing and saving that forces you into saving. Sure, you have had to postpone buying that beautiful new car, but that very delay of gratification will intensify later gratifications.

Look around you and you will see that delaying gratification is a critical factor! It is usually an excellent barometer of one's level of maturity. A child wants everything right now, even if it diminishes something he or she could have later, and of course a child can be forty years old as well as five.

DELAYING GRATIFICATION CRITICAL TO FINANCIAL HEALTH

It is absolutely essential to your financial health to know how to postpone gratification. The nice thing about it is that if you discipline yourself and delay some gratifications, you will benefit in both mental and financial areas.

A certain amount of emotional immaturity exists in us all. The task is slowly to become more mature both mentally and financially—and in every other aspect of our lives.

In the financial world, it really doesn't matter how much you make. It only really matters how much you keep—and that is a matter of discipline, of maturity, of delaying at least some pleasures.

I tell high school and junior high school audiences all the time that if they really are in love with cars, and want to drive a Maserati or a Rolls-Royce, they must postpone gratification now and save money to invest so that they end up with a Rolls-Royce or Maserati. If they delay gratification, they most likely will be able to pay cash for those super luxury cars. And that cash expenditure won't even dent their net worth or liquidity, because by that time they will have developed the habits of saving and carefully controlling and watching their investments.

ACCUMULATE CASH BUT NEVER USE IT

When most people set their financial goals, they write down that they want to make a certain amount of money by a certain date. This is not a bad thing to do, of course, but there is something better. *It doesn't really matter how much money you have, what really is important in the financial world is how much income you derive from the money or assets that you have.* When I was a young stockbroker, one of the other brokers in the office had saved $100,000, which he had put in municipal bonds that gave him a $10,000-a-year income, tax-free, for the next twenty-eight years. And that was without ever touching his own money. The more I thought about that, the more I liked it.

Note that the accumulation of cash is just a means to an end, not the end. You should accumulate cash to put into investments that will generate more cash, so you never have to touch your investment. Instead, you live off the income from that investment, whether it is savings, your own company, property, or discounted paper such as mortgages, trust deeds, or real estate contracts.

CASH IS THE KEY

Cash is really the critical component, more so in tough times than in boom times. But you always need it, so you should always be building reserves through borrowing, as well as through savings. One of the reasons most people don't simultaneously borrow and save is that it isn't easy. It isn't all packaged for them. When you go into a showroom to look at a car, all you have to do is to agree to buy the car and sit down and sign a bunch of papers. The loan documents and all the loan arrangements are made for you. It takes little if any discipline to effectuate and close the deal. But if you are going to borrow money to save (or for that matter borrow money to put down as the initial investment on a deal), you have to take the bull by the horns. You have to take action. You have to make things happen. And negotiating loans with bankers is tough. An ordinary person doesn't just walk off the street into a bank and ask to borrow $15,000 on his or her signature and walk out with the money. It takes more effort than that. You need to stroke the bankers.

STROKING BANKERS

I have found that there are two ways to get your banker to love you. These ways never fail. One is to owe him or her a hundred thousand or two. The other is to lend him a hundred thousand. I can guarantee that if you do either (or preferably both), and if you do it in a small branch of a country bank, every time you walk into that bank, the president or the senior officer will personally greet you. Sure, there are other ways to stroke your banker, but money talks the loudest to him. If you owe him $100,000, he wants to make sure that he's paid back. If you lend him $100,000, he wants to make sure you are happy so you won't pull your money out of his bank and put it in another one. Plus he knows that you might even add to it, which helps all the more.

HOW TO INCREASE YOUR BORROWING POWER

Many people don't think they have the capacity to borrow large sums of money on their signature, so consequently they think they don't have the ability to be liquid. If you first approach banks and other lending institutions for a small loan, it may shock you to see how quickly you can work up to the position of borrowing thousands, tens of thousands, or even more, just on your signature.

The first step might be to borrow a thousand dollars from the bank. If they won't lend that to you on your signature, you could use some collateral with the first loan. But let the banker know that your objective is soon to be able to borrow money without having to put up collateral. After you tell him or her that, go ahead and borrow the first time by putting up collateral. On the first or second loan you might agree to put the money right back into his bank in a savings certificate, using the certificate to collateralize the loan. In this instance, inform the banker that you are doing this to build up your credit with him.

Yes, it will cost you. It will cost you one or two percentage points, but on a thousand dollars that is only one or two hundred dollars a year (and you can borrow the money only for several months, just to take the first step to establish your credit). Again, you want to let the banker know that on subsequent borrowings you will not want to tie the loan to the certificate or to any collateral. The net effect of tying a loan to a certificate is not one of having cash, but to establish your credit. The second or third time you do it, you will end up with, let's say, $2000 in cash in savings and $2000 owed to the bank, with the cash in savings uncollateralized, unattached, and unencumbered in any way, shape, or form.

I would much rather be in the position of having several hundred thousand dollars in my bank account in savings and owing several hundred thousand dollars to the same bank, because in a situation like this (which, incidentally, I have been in many times, good and bad), I am in a position to take advantage of any investment opportunities that come along. In fact, during the last big money crunch I had in excess of half a million dollars in my bank accounts in various types of certificates, and had borrowed an equivalent amount from the bank. This was done as a hedge. If the cash crunch had been devastating, I would have had the flexibility to use the cash to meet emergencies, and/or buy super bargain-basement deals caused by the crunch.

The big bonus to all this was that my credibility with the banks soared. Here we were in a terrible cash crunch throughout the country, and none of the banks that I dealt with had a minute's worth of trouble or worry with me. All loans and notes were paid promptly, and at the same time my balance with each bank was very, very high. I was certainly stroking my bankers, and in a way that they liked to be stroked.

BANKERS ARE JUST JANITORS

That's right! Your banker is just a janitor. He (or she) is a custodian of money, and it's not even his own money. He is caring for somebody else's money, and he is paying rent on it too. That is not to say that he shouldn't be treated with great respect. But you should not be afraid of him. He is not better than you. He is not more powerful than you are. He is just a middleman.

The way to get on his good side is to find out what is most important to him and take care of that need. Core deposits are what he is most interested in. Core deposits are checking accounts. He loves those because it gives him the ability to lend more money to other people, and that is the only way he can make money. He is interested in the size of your core deposit, which is your average daily balance for a month. Every time you go to ask him for a loan, he will punch your account number into the computer to see what your average daily balance is, what kind of interest rate he is going to charge you, and whether he will make you a particular-sized loan.

Since I know his or her methods, I want to have a nice, big, fat average daily balance. It usually pays to deposit a big lump of cash to push up your average daily balance a few weeks or months before asking for a loan. For example, all during January you had an average of only $2000 in your account and you knew that by the first of March you wanted to apply for a loan. The wise thing would have been to transfer any and all excess funds that you had anywhere else into that account during February. Let's say you had deposited an additional $10,000 during February, bringing your total to $12,000. Then your average daily balance would have been much more impressive to the banker when he pulled your statement. Sure, the banker could have gone back and looked at your average daily balance in January, but the statement that he is looking at right now would not include January. And he might or might not go back and look at the January statement.

You might say at this point, "I don't have an extra $10,000 to put in there." But this can be solved in two different ways. First you could borrow money from other banks to increase your core deposit in this bank in order to get an additional loan. Second, you could refer others to your bank and make sure that you get credit for those accounts. If you persuade a relative or friend to transfer his or her account to your bank, make sure that you introduce that person to the bank president or senior officer as he or she opens the account, letting the banker know that it is because of you that the new client is now banking there. In addition, you can drop the banker a letter telling him how much you appreciate the bank and their services and mention that you are responsible for the new account.

For example:

Dear Mr. (Ms.) Banker:

I sincerely appreciate all that your bank does for me and I am very happy with the relationship that we have had for the past _____ years or months. Last week when I brought my friend _____ in, he also expressed his positive feelings at the efficiency of your bank. I think that he will be very pleased banking with you, as I am.

I have several other business associates who are dissatisfied with their banks and I will be bringing them in the next few weeks to introduce them to you.

Again I want to thank you for your bank and the services that it provides.

Sincerely,
Sammy Stroker

You could be accused of manipulation. Call it what you want, but you are giving the banker what he wants, more business, and he eventually will be giving you what you want, the right loans at the right costs.

There are many ways to stroke bankers besides giving them large deposits or business referring to them. There are dinners, luncheons, parties, Christmas and birthday gifts. If you are genuinely interested in them, they will be genuinely interested in you.

Since every bank has a limited amount of funds to lend, they are going to lend money to the person with whom they feel most comfortable and from whom they feel they will have the best chance of getting paid back. If all other factors are even, when they are looking at you and another person and can make only one of you the loan, the extras like dinners, parties, and gifts can make a difference. But don't overdo it. Don't make it obvious or it will seem like a bribe or payoff.

BE TOUGH WITH BANKERS

You need to be tough with bankers, but not mean. You can't let them push you around or they will do it. Don't ever give a banker more collateral than he or she needs. He will keep asking you until you start blinking. So blink early. Know what you have in mind before you sit down. Know what rates to expect to pay, and how much collateral needs to be put up. If you don't know either one of these things, find out. The way to find out is to call people who do a lot of business with banks or even phone rival banks to find the best possible rate you can get on a particular type of loan.

It is always helpful to have a good friend at a competing bank for general information. In fact, this friend might end up competing for your business. Push hard to make sure that your banker understands that you want the best rates and the least amount of collateral you can get away with.

It is also smart to be like your banker. If he has a beard, you grow a beard. If he wears a three-piece suit, you wear a three-piece suit. Don't shock him by your dress or mannerisms. Be what he expects you to be, what he can identify with and trust.

ESTABLISHING TERRIFIC CREDIBILITY

Over and above all else, always do what you say you are going to do. If you borrow money for six months, make sure that it is paid back on the day it is due (or, better yet, early). If the bank calls you and tells you that you have bounced a check, and asks you to come in to cover it, make sure that you are there in the bank that very afternoon. When you say the check is in the mail, make sure that it's in the mail and not sitting there on your desk. Little things like these mean a lot because they add up. You will develop a reputation for being a person of your word on the little things before big things even enter the picture.

Be precise. People will know they can trust your word with exactness rather than having to divide everything you say by two. We all know people who exaggerate any time they give you a figure. If they say they made $25,000 on a deal, you know by experience they have fudged and rounded it off. The only question with these people is whether you need to divide by 2 or 4 or 10.

Most people tend to overstate or overpromise. This decreases their credibility. No one expects you to move the world in a day, so most exaggerations are unnecessary. Don't overpromise. Overpromising pushes you into a corner and makes you seem dishonest. Only promise what you can deliver.

KEEP YOUR BANKER INFORMED

Many times credibility has to be announced. You need to be your own best PR man to let your bankers know what you are doing. Let them know what you and your businesses are doing, how your investments are going.

When you take them to lunch, take them to see your business establishment or investment. Show them the work that is being done. Show them the improvements. Show them statements, pictures, diagrams, projections. Keep them updated. *You* know what is going on, but you have to let *them* know.

If you get an article written about an investment, make several copies and send them to all the key people you deal with so that they also know what is happening. This continues your PR. A simple note attached to the article can do you a lot of good. It could read: "Just thought you would be interested in seeing this article. Thanks to the great support of your bank, I have been able to accomplish this and I am just getting started." You've told them what you are doing, plus you've patted them on the back for the part they played. Everybody is happy.

MORE WAYS TO BUILD CASH RESERVES

Discipline is the key to building cash reserves. I suggest to people who are in a cash crunch to postpone paying some of their bills or spread them out over a much longer period. A typical response is, "Well, if I do that I will probably go ahead and spend the money on something else and I still won't have the bills paid." This shows a lack of discipline.

The concept of pushing back bills of payables, especially during tough times, is one that works and works very well. Many large corporations have been doing it for years. During tough times, delaying payments is much more acceptable to creditors. People who are owed the money are much more reasonable and flexible in working with you because they would rather get paid over a period of time than not at all. They realize that during tough times many companies go out of business and don't pay their bills. But if you don't have the discipline to delay gratification, then you are better off paying the bills now.

People seem to live in two extremes: either they are always

planning for the future and not enjoying the moment or they are indulging themselves right now and do no planning for a future that will almost certainly come. Five or ten years pass very quickly, and without any financial planning you will end up in the same financial situation you are in right at this moment. So use some discipline. Push payables. Delay gratifications in order to intensify them.

If you are pushing payables off into the future, first push those that aren't charging interest. Pay as quickly as possible the ones that are charging the greatest interest. Doing this doesn't have to hurt your credit, especially if you announce to all your creditors that they will get paid, but it will be on a delayed basis. And then be sure to live up to what you promised.

CONSERVING CASH

Years ago, when I was first starting out, an attorney friend of mine told me that I was trying to "poor-boy" it and that by doing so I was going to kill my chances. Not wanting to be tied into a long-term lease, I had rented a small office space on a monthly basis. I furnished it with some secondhand desks and used an old door for a table on which to spread out some of the work. I hired my sister on an hourly basis, and when I got a little bit behind on work, an office temporary. My attorney thought I was making a big mistake. But what I was doing was conserving cash.

Oh, I had cash that I could have put into a plush office, but I wanted that cash to work for me and to work as hard for me as I would work for myself. I knew that if I spent it on cosmetic assets it would take me a lot longer to get where I wanted to go. Too often, people just beginning in the financial world want to look super successful, thinking that having the trappings is the key to success. Many times men and women who have all the outward symbols of success have only leased cars, rented homes, and Master-Charged clothes. The slightest downturn in the economy and this person gets wiped out.

Most wealthy people know how to keep overhead down. Though Aristotle Onassis gave Jacqueline Kennedy a $10-million wedding gift, this was the equivalent of the average person giving a waiter a $20 tip, for at that time Onassis's net worth approached a billion dollars. (The income on that at 10% per year would be $100 million a year without ever touching or spending his own money.) People looking at the $10-million gift don't realize that Onassis used to work for 25 cents an hour for a telephone company in Argentina. He slept in a hovel and worked almost nonstop because he had never before seen anyone get paid by the hour. (In Greece people were paid by the day, and that was sunup to sundown.)

So at the beginning you need to poor-boy it to keep your fixed overhead down to a manageable level. And even when you start to see great progress and growth you need to watch your fixed overhead very carefully because it can get out of hand in a hurry and be the death of a good idea, company, or investment. Virtually every proposed addition to fixed overhead I look at needs to generate a return of at least 2 to 1 within six months or I will have a very hard time justifying adding that expenditure. This includes new employees, specialized equipment, or hired services.

ENCOURAGE OTHERS TO PAY YOU QUICKLY

To build cash liquidity, urge your debtors to pay you quickly. This reduces your collectibles and enhances your position. Incentives, discounts, and bonuses for money coming in early will put you in a strong cash position. Penalties for slow payment work too.

Many companies have added penalties for slow payment without a prior agreement to do so. Corporations, doctors, lawyers, and retail merchants all do it, and people pay it. A typical penalty of 1½% per month on top of the unpaid balance often goes totally unquestioned. If you are being charged 1½% and have not agreed to this penalty in advance, you really don't have to pay it. All you need to do is tell the person or establishment that is charging you that you are not going to pay the penalty because you did not agree to it in advance. This is usually all that it takes to eliminate the charge. On the other hand, in your own business, you might consider adding 1½% per month onto unpaid bills. Do it and see what happens. Sure, some people will complain, but most will pay up without saying a word.

If you have a precise system for collecting money owed to

you, you will find that you will collect a much larger percentage in a much shorter time. Recently I was talking to a president of a collection company in Texas. He told me that on his almost $10 million in yearly collections, his loss is less than 2%. He says that the key is attention to detail and precision in following through on everything that you say you will do, including threats of lawsuits and reports of the bad debt to the credit bureau and Better Business Bureau.

NEGATIVE DOWNPAYMENT

A big problem with cash is that if you use your head you can have thousands, or tens of thousands, and even hundreds of thousands of dollars in savings and checking accounts without having worked for it. You have control over it. You're probably asking, Why is that a problem? Here's why. Because if you are not careful, or if you forget that the cash is not to be spent, a lot of people could get hurt, beginning with you. That cash is sacred and must be held in interest-bearing accounts or invested in assets that are likely to improve in value.

You may not totally believe at this point that it is really quite simple to accumulate large sums of cash. I understand that skepticism because I was that way too. In fact, I was shocked when I read in *The Wall Street Journal* a few years ago about a schoolteacher turned entrepreneur who borrowed $200,000 over the purchase price of an income-producing property. He ended up with $200,000 cash in his pocket, tax-free of course, because it was not an income, it was a loan—and he still owned the property. I was stunned but I was excited too, because I wanted to do the same thing myself. And I did, and did it many times. To my amazement I found that it really wasn't that difficult to do. It just took effort and attention to detail.

But I was soon faced with a tough problem. If I let all this money sit in the bank, I would lose money because the rate that I was borrowing it on was greater than what the bank was paying me on my savings. That's called negative cash flow.

What did I have to do? I had to get that money working so it produced a rate higher than my borrowing cost. But the inviolable rule was that I could not touch those funds.

I solved the cash-flow problem in several ways. On some properties I found a willing buyer who with nothing down would take over the property and pay the high monthly payment in light of the nothing-down deal. (I had already pulled all my cash out, plus it didn't matter to me that they didn't pay me any cash down.) On other properties, I found partners who were willing to feed the negative cash flow as long as I gave them the majority share of the tax benefits, which I did. On yet other properties I took the cash I had generated from such a deal to buy other properties that did produce enough cash flow to feed negative cash flow on the first properties.

Table 2 in Chapter 10 shows six steps by which the so-called negative-down deals can be done where you will end up with substantial cash in your pocket.

10

SUPER-LEVERAGE OR OTHER PEOPLE'S MONEY

OPM—A KEY TO FINANCIAL SUCCESS

Combine other people's money (OPM) with other people's effort (OPE). Add your dream and a workable "system," then stand back and be the financial orchestra conductor. The results will make you, the organizational leader, look small in your own eyes. But the world will think you're great and call you successful.

When I was in my late teens and learning about the stock market, I started to do some OPM daydreaming without even knowing it. I used to think, "Gee, if I could only borrow one hundred dollars from my dad for a month and buy a stock that would go up, I could then sell it, repay my father, and pocket the profit." I reasoned that I could make $15 or $20 in that one-month period, maybe even get lucky and make $40 or $50 without any effort on my part. I then started following some stocks in the paper, pretending to buy them. First, I was hypothetically investing $100 or $200, but then as I became more confident, I would invest thousands and even hundreds of thousands. I got so excited when I made paper profits you would have thought that I had struck the largest oil well in history. But then somebody stuck a pin in my balloon and pointed out two big negatives. First, I would have to pay interest on the money that I borrowed, and second, sometimes stocks actually go down. I've learned since that it is more accurate to say that only once in a while do stocks go up. So I had to go back to the drawing board to refigure my paper profits after deducting out the interest expense, which I did. To my delight, I still had a profit.

LUCK ON LEVERAGE

Later, when I was a stockbroker, I realized that it was indeed tough to pick with any kind of consistency stocks that went up. I also noticed that the ones that did go up were usually sold too soon by the holders, who often missed out on their profits when the stock went the right way. Even though I believed that using other people's money (OPM) was a concept that could make millions for me, I had to find an investment vehicle that I could depend on, one that would increase in value consistently— and I could see stocks were not the answer.

It was at this time that I met Larry Rosenberg. He proved to me that my very elementary concept of OPM did in fact work. He confirmed what I had learned already: you have to be very careful when choosing the investment vehicle that you intend to put your own and other people's money to work in. He had made several million dollars buying distressed assets, using other people's money for the most part. He would take those assets and do something to improve them, increasing their value by 10% or 20%, which would increase his own equity by 100% or 200%!

Most of the assets Larry Rosenberg purchased were real property or income property, primarily apartment buildings. He also did consistently well when buying other assets. He favored real properties because of the control he could exercise over them. He had something to say in what was done with those assets. When buying stocks and bonds, he had to rely upon the expertise and energy of the president and presiding officers of the particular company in which he had invested. In addition, when buying stocks and bonds, he was much more at the mercy of the emotions of the marketplace than he was with real property.

WOULD YOU BELIEVE A 50% RETURN— OR 500%?

OPM, or the use of other people's money, is called financial leverage and it is a critical ingredient for those who start with little or nothing. Just as a long lever can help you lift an object much heavier than yourself, so can a financial lever make you wealthy in a relatively short period of time. Financial leverage can help you achieve rates of return of 50–60–70% and more.

YOU JUST INHERITED $50,000

Let me give you an example of how financial leverage works. Suppose you have just inherited $50,000 and decide to use it to purchase a home for that amount. But a year later something comes up and you have to move. Inflation has increased the value of your home by 10%, so you put your house on the market for $55,000. Assuming, for simplicity, that you sold the house yourself and there were no closing costs, when the sale is closed, you put your $5000 profit in your pocket and happily go on your way.

But most of us don't have $50,000 cash, so we use the great principle of financial leverage. Instead of the $50,000, suppose you have only $5000. You pay $5000 down on a house and borrow the balance from the bank (or preferably from the seller or a combination of the seller and a bank). Again, a year later, you have to sell the house. Again, it is worth $55,000. But this time when you sell it things are much different.

10% WITH LEVERAGE EQUALS 100%

Instead of making 10% on your money, you make a whopping, and, to some people, an unbelievable, 100%. How can this be? Surely I made a mistake in figuring!

But of course I didn't make a mistake. You put up $5000 and a year later you sold the house for $55,000, giving you a net profit of $5000. You get all of your initial $5000 back as well, so that equals a 100% return on your investment dollar.

LIFTING MORE WITH LEVERAGE

How can the same house yield a 100% return in one case and only 10% in the other? The answer is what financial leverage is all about. *Financial leverage is the process of using other people's money to enhance your own financial position.* Obviously, when you borrow $45,000, there are interest costs that would alter the figures I have presented. But keep in mind that when buying a house or another type of asset that produces income from rents, leases, or profits, those profits or rents can be used to pay the interest as well as pay down on the balance of the loan.

Houses or real estate are not the only way you can make this leverage work. There are many ways that you can use this same principle to increase your financial position by 50% to 100% every year. This can be done over and over again with great consistency.

HOW DOES LEVERAGE WORK?

What makes leverage work? Why is it that with other people's money your own money can multiply at a synergistic rate?

First, we need to see why money is available for us to use as leverage. There are millions of people in this country who love to put their money into banks, credit unions, savings and loan institutions, and insurance companies.

In exchange for the use of their money, those institutions give the saver a 5% return (or whatever current rates are). Then the banks lend the money out at 8% to 18% to businesses and individuals who are willing to make the effort to work for even higher rates of return.

So an individual can borrow money at, say, 12% and put it to work for him for a 50% return. His or her net return, on someone else's money, is 38%.

How does leverage work, then? Let's look at an example. Suppose you have $1000 and you borrow an additional $9000 from the bank at 10% interest. If your investment yields an 11% return, you'll receive a net return of $200 dollars.

11% return on $10,000	$1,100
10% interest cost on $9,000	$ 900
Net Profit	$200

That $200 is a 20% return on your initial $1000. What brought it about? You received 11% on your own money ($110), plus you received 1% (11% return minus 10% interest), resulting in ninety dollars on other people's money.

What if you were to make the same investment and have a 20% overall return, which is very reasonable? Then you'd be making $900 on that money from the bank, instead of just $90.

And that's $900 after you have paid off the interest you owe them! Add that to the $200 you'd make on your own money and your total would be $1100 profit, or 110% return on a 20% increase in value of the asset you bought. Not bad!

THE SPREAD, NOT THE COST OF "BREAD," IS THE KEY

Borrowing money at 10%, lending it out at 11%, gives you only a 1% "spread," which is a tight margin and would not normally be recommended. You should look for much larger spreads than that.

IT'S THE "I" AND THE "U" THAT MAKE OPIUM A GOOD ADDICTION

OPIUM becomes addictive when you realize that you have to add "I," or yourself, and "U," the other person, to OPM. Both parties have to have their needs met. When you do this, you can work wonders, for by adding the "I" and the "U" you turn OPM into OPIUM and will be addicted for life. You see, "I" have to get money at a reasonable rate in order to make money on whatever appreciating asset I am investing in, and "U" have to receive enough interest (for your passive investments) to entice you to let me use your money.

People are constantly asking me at seminars how much they should pay for borrowed money. The answer to that depends on how much return they expect with a reasonable degree of assurance. Let's say you are buying a $275,000 building for 10% down ($27,500), and you know that when you finish fixing the building at an additional cost of, let's say, $25,000, the building will be worth $400,000 (net of sales commission and all closing costs). If the money you need to borrow for the downpayment and the fix up of the property will cost you 25% per annum, the purchase of such property is still a deal and a very good deal.

Here's why. You have a $400,000 asset net of sales commission and closing costs, which gives you an equity of $150,-000—$400,000 less $250,000—owing on the balance of the mortgage. Your total borrowed down and borrowed fix-up costs investment is $52,500. In other words you made almost a 300% return on those short-term dollars you borrowed to buy and to fix up the building. So to pay 25% on the $52,500 would not be excessive. In fact, that would only be $13,125 in a one-year period. So how much would you net on this entire transaction? You would have a $150,000 profit from which you would have to deduct $25,000 fix-up money, $27,500 down-payment, which you borrowed, and $13,125 interest-carrying cost for the two foregoing loans, a total of $65,625 expenses, which leaves you a grand total of $84,375 profit. And you didn't put up a single dollar of your own money. What you did put up, however, was your ability to recognize opportunity and just as important, your courage to do something about it, even though there were some risks (which there always are).

MR. AND MRS. SELLER CAN BE YOUR BEST BANKERS

In many areas of the country the bankers have pushed individuals a little too far. They have made loan agreements too complicated, too costly, and too restrictive on other assets. Consequently, we have seen some great changes in financing and no doubt we will continue to see those changes as time goes on.

BUYING A BUSINESS WITH ITS OWN CASH

Here is what is happening. Let's say that John and Mary Doe, age sixty-five and sixty-three respectively, have owned a small, profitable business for many years. (This example could apply equally well to real property, an office building, a warehouse, a shopping center, a medical building or an apartment building.) They have owned this profitable business long enough to have cleared off all long- and short-term debt. But they are tired and they want out. Their sons and daughters have gone their various ways and none have an interest in running the business, and the owners really don't want another person to manage it.

What they really want is to sell it. You come along and are a willing buyer. Their price sounds fine. In addition to that, you know that you can make the business even more profitable because of your ability to recognize trends and what people want right now. You're excited, and you want it badly. They are asking $265,000 for the business. You have got $20,000 in savings and $30,000 in equity in your own home. You go to the bank and ask for a loan to finance the balance. You are willing to put up almost everything you own because you are that sure that you can make the business even a bigger winner than it already is. The bank agrees to lend you only $100,000 of the $265,000 purchase price. No matter how hard you push for a larger loan, you finally realize that $100,000 is their top. Just when you have lost all hope, the sellers offer to let you owe them the balance of $145,000 as long as you are willing to secure a small part of that by giving them a second-trust deed on the equity on your home. You quickly and gladly agree and the deal is done. Basically, first-, second-, third-, etc., trust deeds as well as first, second, third, etc., mortgages on the same property differ from one another simply by the order in which they are filed at the county recorder's office. The documents themselves are exactly the same (for the same property). The numbers "first," "second," "third," etc., constitute the pecking order of liens or foreclosures.

Transactions like this one are a common occurrence these days. Naturally, the seller has to be asked and/or persuaded to carry the second financing, but he is now doing this in record numbers. Sometimes the second loan carried by the seller has a lower interest rate than the bank loan. The buyers who are taking advantage of this less expensive financing with easier terms are reaping financial windfalls.

ARE YOU MISSING OUT ON THIS FINANCIAL BANDWAGON?

Businesses, income properties, and other types of appreciating assets that are free and clear of all debt are the most likely candidates for this kind of financing. If loans exist against the businesses or properties, secondary financing can still be carried by the seller. Recently, a banker told me he couldn't make money with only a 3% spread. If he paid 9% on his money and lent it out at 12%, the situation was not profitable for his bank. Why? Because of administrative costs in between. You eliminate those costs almost totally when you deal on a person-to-person basis. With banks able to pay interest rates on your checking account balances, you just know that the cost of money is going to go even higher. Unless there are some radical changes, the process of financing between two parties, eliminating banks and other financial institutions, will continue to grow. If you are not participating, you are missing out on a real financial bandwagon.

FOR THOSE IN A HURRY FOR BIG BUCKS

Conrad Hilton's mother told him, "If you want to launch big ships, you have to go where the water is deep." If you want to get to your financial destination in a big hurry, you have to take larger risks. The following is a technique for benefiting handsomely from those risks. And as you will see, you can actually shift the risk to someone else.

SIX STEPS TO SUPER-LEVERAGE

The following six steps and accompanying Table 2 illustrate how the super-leverage process works. These six steps will show you how to put either $62,500 or $42,500 in your pocket and still own the property. Rather than doing all of this at the time of closing, it is done in a more simple manner by first buy-

Table 2

STEP #1

$100,000
−20,000
$80,000   balance on a first-trust deed or real estate contract
9%, 30 years. Fifteen-year balloon
Monthly payment $644.

STEP #2

Improve property or business with $10,000 cash
New value $150,000
How Can You Get Maximum Cash Out?

STEP #3

Arrange tentative loan 75% of value = $112,500
(*Get written commitment*)

STEP #4

Approach former owner—sweeten his terms

Original Deal

$100,000
$-20,000$
$ 80,000

9%, 30 years. Fifteen-year balloon

Alternative #1	*Alternative #2*
10% interest	11% interest
$20,000 payoff	$40,000 payoff
Ten-year balloon	Five-year balloon

Whatever he agrees to, get him to
sign an agreement!

STEP #5

Go back to source that agreed to loan $112,500 (Step #3). When they fund the loan they will automatically pay off your $80,000 balance directly to former owner.

Loan proceeds $112,500
                    $-80,000
                    $32,500   *Cash to you*

STEP #6

Set up closing with seller to execute second-loan papers. (He gives you a check, you sign the loan document.)

Alternative #1		*Alternative #2*
Total mkt. value	$150,000	$150,000
First mortgage or loan	112,500	112,500
Second mortgage or loan	60,000	40,000
Cash in pocket	$92,500	$72,500
After refinancing		Cash Back
		Less down $20,000
		Fix-up exp. 10,000
Total	$62,500	$42,500

ing the property and later (whether that is one month or six months or a year) effectuating the phase 2 described in the six steps. It can be done all at the closing, but one must have a very aggressive and open-minded banker.

USE THE SAME CONCEPT ON JOHN AND MARY DOE DEAL

When John and Mary Doe sold you a $265,000 business (See "Buying a Business With Its Own Cash," page 138), and agreed to carry back a big hunk of the financing, they really did you a favor and allowed you to own something that you ordinarily would not have been able to buy. It would have been an even sweeter deal if they had agreed to lend you the entire purchase price, less your downpayment. In both cases you stand to win, especially if you make the business run as well as you thought you could.

But believe it or not, the best is really yet to come, if you take a few steps to improve your position. Let's take the example of a $100,000 asset (business or income-producing property) and see what big advantages we can come up with *after* the initial sale, whether it is one month later or a year later. Table 2 gives six steps to super leverage.

STEP 1: BUY AND OWE THE SELLER

In Step 1, a $100,000 property or business is bought with a 20%, ($20,000) downpayment, leaving an $80,000 balance secured by a first trust deed or on real estate contract. That contract is owed to the seller. The terms of that loan are 9%/thirty years with a balloon payment that makes the entire sum due and payable after the fifteenth year. The monthly payment is $644. So you now have purchased the asset and are holding it. The $20,000 downpayment on the asset could be cash that you had or have borrowed.

STEP 2: INCREASE VALUE WITH IMPROVEMENTS

In Step 2, you improve the property or business with $10,000 cash influx. If it is a business that we are talking about, by adding $10,000 with some very wise and strategic marketing, you could increase the profitability of the business and hence increase the value of the business. Likewise, with an income-producing property, by making physical and/or managerial changes we are assuming that you increase the value to $150,000 (See Chapter 7: "How Yuks Can Create Big Bucks").

STEP 3: OBTAIN REFINANCING COMMITMENT

Now, to get the maximum cash out of the asset, in Step 3 you approach a lending institution and ask them to evaluate and appraise the business or property since you want to borrow against that asset. It is wise to have an independent appraisal done of the asset before you approach the bank so you can go in with your guns loaded and show the banker on paper exactly what you think it is worth with the studied opinion of at least one other professional party who has evaluated it. Assuming they agree to make the loan, get a written commitment from the lending institution. In this case, the written commitment would be $112,500.

STEP 4: SWEETEN TERMS TO SELLER

In Step 4, which is probably the most critical one, you approach the former owner and offer him a deal that will benefit both of you. In other words, you sweeten the terms that you originally agreed to. Remember, you owe the seller $80,000 to be paid over thirty years at 9%. So you say to the fellow, I want to change the terms of the loan I owe you and make them better for you, and if I do this for you, there's something that you can do for me. What you want him to do is to "subordinate" his position, to move his first-loan position into a second-loan position, behind and "subordinate to" the new loan that you have lined up from the bank. All "subordinate" means is that his loan is now in a junior position to the first loan, which means that if the property were ever in default and foreclosure procedure were to take place, the first position with the loan to the bank would be paid first and whatever was left over would be paid to the second position.

You may very well ask at this point, who in their right mind would agree to subordinate his position this way and why? When I first read of this technique in *The Wall Street Journal* some years ago, I asked the same question. It didn't seem plausible to me that any sane person would move into an obviously weaker position. But people were doing it, so why shouldn't I give it a try?

I found to my amazement that many people were willing to subordinate their position if it was put to them in the right way and if the benefits were fair to them. My belief in the technique was strengthened when I found that Ray Kroc and McDonald's Corporation had used a variation of this technique in their beginning stages when they were short of cash. It became the major contributing factor to McDonald's fantastic growth.

One of the keys to getting the former owner to accept the deal is to sweeten his terms enough so that he sees something in it for him to make it worthwhile to take the risk.

You can be creative in sweetening terms. For instance, raise interest rates; increase the amount of collateral; throw in round-trip tickets somewhere (this seems to be especially effective with women); give him a boat or some other gift.

Probably just as important is for you to convince him or her that you are trustworthy. Here is where a good solid reputation can mean the difference between success and failure. Be straightforward, make sure he sees that in alternative #1 he is exposed to the tune of $22,500 and in alternative #2 his exposure is $2500. Since the total mortgages add up to $172,-500 in alternative #1 and $152,500 in alternative #2, in case of default and subsequent foreclosure the seller would be exposed or would lose $22,500 and $2500 respectively, assuming that the property was sold for the same market value of $150,000.

Let's say, for the sake of example, that you offer the seller alternative #1. You raise the interest rate in alternative #1 to 10% versus 9% he is currently receiving and offer to pay him a $20,000 balloon payoff at the time you close the new loan, and then you also offer to shorten the balloon from fifteen to ten years. If alternative #1 doesn't work, then you sweeten the terms even further as shown in alternative #2. Whatever he agrees to, get him to sign that agreement.

Have your attorney draft a simple agreement. (I stress "simple" in order not to scare the former seller away.) Knowing that the word "simple" doesn't seem to be in an attorney's vocabulary, many times I have drawn up a simple agreement in letter form myself. Make sure that there is a meeting of the minds. Make sure that he understands what you are doing. Don't try to pull the wool over his eyes. Frankness is the best way to avoid hassles or a court fight later on. (See Chapter 14 on Avoiding Financial Traps.)

STEP 5: HAVE BANK FUND THE LOAN

After the former owner has agreed to subordinate his or her position, you go back to the source that agreed to loan you the $112,500 in Step #3. When they fund the loan, they will automatically pay off your $80,000 balance that you owe directly to the former owner, which will leave you $32,500.

STEP 6: FINALLY

Now in the final step, Step 6, you merely execute the final procedures that you agreed upon. The former seller has the $80,-000 in his hand, and you have a loan of $112,500 on the asset. You meet with him at his home, office, or a third party's office and he gives you, as per the agreement, a check for either $60,000 or $40,000, depending upon which alternative he agreed to ($80,000 less the $20,000 or $40,000 you agreed to reduce the loan by). You sign the loan documents and walk away with a total of $62,500 or $42,500 in your pocket. As you can see from Table 2, in Step 6 (alternative #1), you now have a property or business or income property which has $172,500 loan against it, or $152,500 in loans in alternative #2. And you still own the property.

In both cases you have more in loans against the property than the total market value of the property, and in either case you would have a negative cash flow. Now if you were to go out and spend this money on "adult toys" or trips around the world or the like, you would end up with a real problem. But if you use the cash wisely, reinvesting in the business or property or buying other appreciating assets that generate income, you should be able to feed the negative cash flow generated by the sizable loans against the assets.

WHAT IF THE SELLER SAYS NO?

If the seller will not agree to either alternative #1 or #2, there are many other options to offer him or her. For example, you could formally agree to put more cash into the property or business to make the asset worth even more; or, to secure his exposed position, you could even give him additional collateral by putting up other buildings, or businesses, or your home.

WHAT SHOULD YOU TELL THE BANK?

You also wonder about how to handle the bank. Is the bank that is lending the first loan going to agree to the subordinate second? The answer to that is, it depends. It depends upon you and your relationship with the banker. It also depends on whether the bank is aggressive or highly conservative. You may choose not to disclose to the lending institution your intention to put additional loans on the property. After all, they really shouldn't care, since they are in first position and in case of default they wouldn't have any trouble getting their money back. It is, however, far better to let the bank know what you're doing. How you tell them can be important. An "Oh, by the way, I'm putting a second loan on that property and I thought you'd like to be kept current on my business" is a much better approach than asking the bank for permission.

If the papers you signed to borrow the money from the bank did not obligate you to make this disclosure, then I see no reason to tell them. However, many loan agreements have clauses that say you cannot encumber the property without their permission.

Some people use the foregoing super leverage technique to generate large amounts of cash and then sell those over-leveraged assets to competent, energetic managers whose efforts increase the cash flow to at least cover the negative cash flow. Thus, they free themselves to make other deals.

Anyone who chooses to go this route needs to keep close tabs on those assets that he or she has sold or turned over to specialists to manage. You would not want to get in the position of defaulting on any of those loans. Your financial reputation is worth a lot more than whatever cash you would generate from a few properties.

BUYING A BUSINESS WITH ITS OWN CASH

Income properties can be bought with their own future cash in the form of rental income. Or, in cases where you buy well under the true market value, those properties can be purchased with their own present cash by refinancing.

Likewise, in buying a business you can pay for that business with its own future profits, and, in many cases, as Meshulam

Riklis showed in his book *The Magic of Mergers,* from cash that is just sitting in the company. Riklis and others have actually bought small, medium, and large corporations for less cash than the company being bought had in its own till.

11

SMART MONEY HEDGES FOR BAD TIMES

SMART MONEY HEDGES BETS WHEN TOUGH TIMES ARE COMING

Wouldn't anybody hedge his bet if he knew that tough times were coming? Of course he would; but the average guy doesn't know that tough times are coming. Smart money is never certain either, but there are indications that give him a head start on everyone else. No, he is not always right, but most of the time he is. The most important ingredient for recognizing the approach of tough times is to be an independent thinker, a person who looks at the entire picture and avoids being unduly influenced by outside sources, unless one or two sources have proven to be uncannily accurate for many years. What does the smart money look at? The big picture. Smart money looks at *trends*.

THE ECONOMIC RIVER

"Trends" is a very important word to an independent thinker. The overall economy is like a gigantic river. Sure, you can swim upstream, but it is very difficult. What smart money does is watch the *general direction* of the flow of that giant stream. Smart-money people know that the flow doesn't suddenly turn around and move the other way.

Some sectors of the economy can make quicker reversals than others, but even here there are trends. Interest rates, for example, can start moving quickly upward or downward, but usually you can spot even interest-rate movements if you take the time to observe. I always pay a lot more attention to the trends in consumer-confidence polls than I do to polls taken of economists' ideas of what will happen in the future, because my observation has shown me that the consumer-confidence polls are more accurate. The consumer will start buying more personal goods and being more confident as the economy turns, before he has enough belief in a major recovery to invest in property, new businesses, or even stocks.

As we pulled out of the last recession, which was deep and long, I was surprised to note that six people in my own relatively small office all indicated in one month that they were in the market for a new car. That told me something. It told me that there was new confidence that the recession was ending or had already ended.

PLAY BOTH SIDES

When smart money encounters real tough times, bets are hedged, just as a smart person or corporation hedges when donating political funds. If you needed the cooperation of the local zoning commission, and the commissioner in charge of zoning were running for election and it looked like a close race, smart money would donate to both candidates. You can't lose. Likewise, you can bet on both sides much of the time if you stop to figure out just exactly how to do it.

Many bright entrepreneurs anticipated the great liquidity crunch and the record-breaking high interest rates that hit in the early 1980s. So they began to take steps to hedge their bets. They certainly didn't want to terminate their businesses, but they didn't want to be put out of business for lack of cash either. So they started building cash reserves. (See Chapter 9: "Cash Coming Out of Your Years.") They reasoned that even if they were wrong and cash didn't become a very dear commodity and interest rates didn't go sky high, they would still not be in a disastrous position. If they were right but failed to build big cash reserves, that lack of cash could force them out of business. So they built their cash position, using many of the techniques that I will talk about in this chapter.

PAPER PROPERTIES

Another way to hedge your bets, one that is being done more and more, is by buying "paper" instead of, or in addition to, property or a business. "Paper" represents any document secured by a property that pays you on a predetermined basis. Buying "paper" properties is like buying up the IOUs of others—their mortgages and loans. They are high-yield assets. In the early eighties many people saw that large profits could be made if Reaganomics was successful and caused inflation and consequently interest rates to drop substantially and remain low. This opportunity for hedging one's long-term bet is still open. It is an opportunity spawned by the large amount of activity occurring in the past years in buying and selling real property (single-family homes, multiple apartment buildings, and other commercial types of improved properties).

With high interest rates, many buyers and sellers could not transact their deals because of lack of normal institutional financing. Consequently, many sellers found themselves carrying some of the buyers' financing themselves, even though they didn't want to. There are thousands of people who have sold homes and other real estate properties who are currently holding unwanted second mortgages or trust deeds as well as real estate contracts. Since these people really don't want to hold these notes, they (may) qualify as motivated sellers. But this time they are motivated sellers of paper properties. If you buy these notes at the right price, the return on your invested dollar can be tremendous. Let me give you an example.

28% RETURN WITHOUT FIXING TOILETS

Say Motivated Marvin is trying to sell his home and is unable to do so because everybody wants to buy it with only a very low downpayment, and Motivated Marvin is insistent about getting all of his cash out. After months and months of trying to sell it, Marvin realizes that he is not going to be able to do it without making some concessions, so he finally sells the house by carrying back or financing some of the paper himself. He agrees to hold a $25,000 second-trust deed or mortgage for twenty years at a 14% rate, but he insists on a five-year balloon, i.e., the entire amount of the note is payable within five years. So there sits Marvin with a second mortgage or trust deed that he doesn't want. He couldn't get the cash he wanted. Now you enter the picture. You offer him cash for his note, cash that he can have now and that he doesn't have to wait five years to receive. Of course you don't offer him the full face value of the $25,000 note. Instead you offer to buy him out only if he will accept a discount, and a deep one at that.

You offer him $12,500, or fifty cents on the dollar. Assume he is sufficiently motivated because he needs the cash and he needs it now. He accepts your offer. Let's examine where that puts you. You now own a note that is secured by real property which pays you a current yield of approximately 28%, which isn't a bad yield even if rates were to stay high or to rise to the record levels that they were a few years ago. What you are counting on—at least this is the reason for the hedge—is the possibility that rates will slide even further than they have to record low levels again. If rates did slide, there you would be sitting with a very fat yield of 28% while others had to be satisfied with very skinny yields.

But let's assume that you are wrong and rates go back up. Has this hedge really hurt you that badly? The answer to that is an emphatic NO, because if rates do continue being pushed up by inflation, the underlying property that secures your loan is obviously worth more and more each year. Within a short time, if history repeated itself, you would find that someone would eventually refinance the property, and upon refinancing, would have to cash you out. Now when it comes to cashout time, there you are sitting with a $25,000 note even though you only paid $12,500 for it. It will be cashed out at its face value unless you were to negotiate something less than that—which of course you shouldn't be very anxious to do. Even though this is a hedge, you could actually end up winning very big on either side of the hedge.

If you were to do the math, you would see that if you were cashed out, you would not only have received 28% yield along the way, but you would have doubled your cash investment immediately and made 100% in addition to the 28% per year for whatever number of years you held it.

MORE, MORE, MORE

But that's not all. If you didn't have any cash at the time that you bought the paper property, you could go out and borrow the money and use other people's money to make it a total leverage situation for yourself—a leverage situation that did not cost you any time or effort once you bought the investment.

Assuming you have paid 15% for the borrowed money, you would still be making 13% on other people's money. So for every $100,000 worth of paper you buy like this, you would have $13,000 income, and that is passive income. You would not have to fix toilets or collect rents. All you would have to do is to receive a monthly check, make out a deposit slip, make the deposit, and make payment on the underlying financing that you received from the bank. I don't know about you but, for more than $1000 a month, I'll do that any day.

Remember that this is a hedge and it is usually done in combination with buying properties, so either way you can win. There are people who buy nothing but so-called discounted paper and make a very handsome living doing just this.

THE PAPER CHASE

How do you find motivated sellers of paper? Several ways. (1) By running your own ads, advertising that you are a willing buyer with cash to buy first mortgages, second mortgages, and real estate contracts. (2) By referrals. Tell other people what you do and ask them to spread the word. One of the better referral systems is through real estate brokers and agents because many times they have deals that wouldn't go through if it were not for someone who was waiting in the wings to buy the piece of paper that is generated by the closing. Even bankers can be a good source of leads, particularly mortgage bankers and the loan officers who work in the mortgage departments of banks. Some savings and loans have been quick to pick up on this method, but usually most individual buyers have it head and shoulders above banks when it comes to knowing how to negotiate in order to get those very handsome yields.

Of course negotiating is a very big part of it. You need to take time to learn how to negotiate and negotiate hard so as to get the top yields for your own paper portfolio. Follow this method very far and it is like opening your own bank. In fact you are in the financing business, and in many ways acting just like a bank. You'll have much higher spreads than most banks are used to, plus you have the bonus of having much lower overhead—at least if you are smart.

SUBJECT TO . . .

Other things smart money can do to hedge in tough and/or in anticipation of tough times includes the use of options; that is, tying up properties and businesses and other appreciating assets with a minimal amount of money on an option basis. An option is a piece of paper or contract that gives you the right to choose within a fixed period of time whether you want to buy a property or business at a set price. Obviously you have to pay something for these options, but they can be negotiated at a very low price, which gives you a hedge against what will happen. For example, if a property or business were for sale but times were tough or on the way there, and you were to pay $5000, that would give you time to see how bad things were going to be. In fact, if the option is long enough, say, six months or a year—the bad times could lift and you could then exercise the option to buy the property or the business for the price agreed upon when the market was low.

I've seen long-term "subject-to" clauses used for the same purpose without any cost to the buyer. The subject-to clause says in essence that the offer to buy the property is good "only if" the buyer accepts the physical and/or financial condition (or whatever condition he or she wishes to put in there) of the property or business. This can have any time limit that the purchaser wishes to put on it. In the meantime the property is off the market. No one else can buy it. Many times, the seller is so anxious to sell that a long-term offer with a strong subject-to clause will be accepted, in effect giving the buyer a free option.

BACKUP PLANS FOR BOTTOMING OUT

Smart money seems always to be considering hedges or at least alternatives. Gordon Walker of McLean, Virginia, an entrepreneur currently on a special Presidential appointment has been very successful using this philosophy. He says that he always plans on failing. Not that he thinks he is going to fail, but he always has a backup plan just in case things do go wrong.

In addition to this philosophy, Walker thinks that most smart money and most smart people do one thing and do it well. "Find your own niche," he says. "I don't think that there is just one smart way to do something. There are many. But you do need to find a niche and know it and know it well and stay there.'' He goes on to say that you should be bigger than the little guys and smaller than the big guys. In preparing for failure he emphasizes, for example, that you try to get nonrecourse loans. A nonrecourse loan is one in which the lender has recourse, if you default on the loan, only against the property, not against you personally, so that if a business venture fails, you won't be obligated to pay personally. That is a smart-money hedge. That kind of flexibility can get you out of some very bad spots.

What are other smart-money people doing? Steve Blaser, owner of a million-dollar-a-year mobile-home sales operation, says, ''I never expand when business is good, only when business is bad.'' Most people begin to pull in when business is bad, but Blaser believes that expansion makes sense at that time because people are hungry and anxious for jobs.

Mr. Blaser has a point. In fact, he's following Baron Rothschild's axiom to buy ''when there is blood in the streets.''

He is going against the grain and doing his own thinking. It has paid off for him, too. Since starting from scratch ten years ago, he's now the largest dealer in his state.

What did he do when times got tough? He expanded because he had the cash, and he had the cash because he was bright enough and he was independent enough to see what was coming and take the necessary steps to ensure that he would have cash.

That's what smart money does in tough times. They are always thinking, they are always going against the crowd, and the rewards are waiting for them.

12

OTHER PEOPLE'S EFFORTS

OPE GROWTH THROUGH BUILDING GIANT MEN AND WOMEN TO BUILD YOUR GIANT NET WORTH

Combine other people's money (OPM) with other people's effort (OPE) and the results can be nothing short of phenomenal. Few people ever take the time to calculate what can happen in a short period of time through numbers. The geometric progression is something that can be absolutely stunning.

If you hired ten people to work for you and each of them were to hire ten more and those people were to solicit the efforts of ten more people each, you would have 1110 helping you accomplish whatever was your set task.

All of us are limited in what we can do because our time is limited. Any large organization, private or public, could not have attained its size without this concept of OPE, other people's efforts. To do anything in a big way requires other people's help. Besides, when you do something big, it's a lot more fun to share those great feelings of accomplishment.

YOU CAN'T SEEM TO FIND BAD HELP ANYMORE

One cliché that you and I have heard, especially when talking to people with small businesses, is, "You can't find good help anymore." But if that is true, isn't it amazing how many companies have grown to highly successful and profitable ventures in the last few years? For some unknown reason they have been able to hire many topnotch men and women who have enhanced the company. Few people would argue that if you had a bunch of good people surrounding you and carrying out your dreams and your tasks, you would be able to accomplish much more than if you tried to do it yourself.

After having hired and fired many people in the last ten years, I've learned that it takes a lot of work and effort and even some luck to hire the right person for the right job. You have to remember that no one is ever perfect. Even if you are looking at executives and employees of other companies who are excellent and seem like "the best," when you see them up close, you'll see that they too have weaknesses, faults, and flaws. You also have to realize that the boss usually expects someone else to do a job exactly as he or she would do it, which is not a realistic expectation. At times your employees won't do a job as well and at times they will do it better. But almost all the time, they will do it differently.

TWENTY-SIX-YEAR-OLD HAS 200,000 PEOPLE WORKING FOR AND WITH HIM

The multilevel marketing companies have quickly learned the power of OPE. Companies like AMWAY make a big to-do about OPE and its effects, and of course they are right. If you set up a system in which people work hard for you and are benefiting themselves at the same time, you can be on easy street in a short time. But you must get the right people for the right jobs. In building your own organization, be sure to spend plenty of time selecting the right personality for a particular position. This is critical.

Young Mark Hughes saw the power in the OPE concept. At the age of twenty-six he heads up a multimillion-dollar company that he started himself. How did he move the company from one million to fifty-five million in gross sales three years later? You guessed it. Through OPE. He now has over 200,000 distributors selling products for Herbal Life International Inc., based out of Culver City, California. You can bet that he found people who were worth hiring, and I would be willing to wager that he hired a sizable number of people who were a lot smarter than he is.

The problem with many of us is that we let our egos get in

the way. We want to be the smartest one or seem to be the smartest one in our own organization. Just remember: it's impossible to play all the positions on football, basketball, or baseball teams at the same time. Business organizations are teams too. So what are the keys to effective hiring?

HIRE A WAITRESS AND SHARE DREAMS AND PROFITS

First of all, realize that whatever business you are involved in, you are in the people business. If you build people, they will build you. Second, always be looking for good people to hire or to associate with no matter what business or position they are in—salesclerk, waitress, or racecar driver. Third, share your dreams and goals as well as your profits with the men and women who work with you. Remember, the key word in all this is the preposition "with." People don't work *for* you nearly as hard as when they work *with* you. Fourth, let your employees be themselves. Let their unique personalities benefit your organization. This means that they need to be put in places where they can contribute the most. An accountant-type personality is usually not meant to be a super salesman and vice versa.

EASY TO HIRE JUST ANYBODY

Realize that your most important task is hiring the right people, which is almost a full-time job in itself. The interviewing process is a waste of time unless you put some real effort into it because during an interview anybody is going to tell you the best story about himself that he can. He is going to do nothing but build himself up and make himself look as good as he can in your eyes, which of course is only right. Personality, attitude, and skill-level tests are all good, but they are at best only indications. An interview is only an indication, but if you probe deeply enough many times you can get closer to the truth.

THREE KEYS TO HIRING THE RIGHT PERSON FOR THE RIGHT JOB

Assuming that you know exactly the position that you are trying to fill and the type of person you need to fill it, I find the best source of potential candidates is people who are already working and are happy in their present positions. Top people are usually not trying to find a job. When I am looking for a person to fill a position, I get on the phone and ask friends and business associates whom they know that is the very best in a particular position I am trying to fill. In addition to referrals from others, my own observations rate high on my list. *It is much more important to observe how people work and react than how they talk.*

The second key is to ask the right questions in several interviews that you conduct with potential employees. Most job candidates will answer what they think you want to hear because they want the job. If you ask if someone is highly organized, it will be obvious to him or her that organization is important in the particular position. Of course he is going to say that he is a good organizer. But if you give him a list of five traits—for example, organizational ability, follow-through ability, working with people, decision-making, and skill at filling out forms, and ask him to pick the one he is best at, this question forces him to choose just one. After he indicates this strongest skill, ask him what he thinks he is second-best at, and third, fourth, and fifth. If organizational ability ends up on the bottom you know you have a problem.

There are two hard-to-measure traits that I am always looking for in people: energy level and initiative. I can usually get an indication of how strong a person is here by giving him a list of eight to ten traits along with these two and asking him to rate himself on a scale from 1 to 10 on each one.

Many times I will interview the candidate along with his/her spouse. I normally ask the spouses how they rate their husband or wife in those traits that seem to be so hard to measure by testing. All of these, of course, give me a general indication of the person's skill, attitude, and general interest level. Naturally, if a job candidate says he's energetic and his background is totally void of accomplishments, you have reason to doubt.

The last and very critical key is reference checking. Normally, the only significant references are those from former employers. Personal references and character references obviously are friends who will invariably give nothing but "As" and "A+s" to the applicant. In checking references, one must probe deeply and ask tough questions of former employers. There are very few employers who want to say bad things about a former employee, even if he or she fired the person. So ask questions such as, "Why did you fire her?" "Would you rehire him in the same position right now?" Then listen very carefully to any possible hesitations in giving the recommendations. Ask the reference to give a list of all the former employee's strengths as well as a list of weaknesses. Get him or her to prioritize critical traits just as you would while interviewing the candidate himself or herself.

DON'T HESITATE TO FIRE SOMEONE

Baron Rothschild remarked that the hardest part of managing was firing people, and that the only managerial mistake he ever made was waiting too long to fire someone. I would quickly and loudly echo that sentiment. If you are going to hire, you have to be willing to fire, because no one picks the perfect employee for the job every time. You will make some mistakes. You are not doing anyone any favors by postponing your decision to let him or her go. Yes, it is very painful. It is a piece of cake to hire and a pain in the neck to fire. But it must be done. Once you have made the decision to fire someone, be sure to follow through with it immediately. Don't be talked out of it regardless of tears, threats, or guilt feelings that you may have to face during or after the termination meeting.

If someone is not working out in a position, the first thing I examine is whether the position fails to fit the person. If that is the case, I try to move the person to a place that fits him/ her. I have done this several times with great success. In one case I moved a top executive several times before I found the niche that fitted him to a "t." If the employee has a good attitude and is willing to work, it's well worth the time to try to find the right place for him, for his benefit and yours.

Most of the time your gut feeling about how a person is doing on the job is right. We have a tremendous capacity to communicate in so many ways other than orally. Our subconscious mind picks up so much from body language, off-the-cuff remarks, and even a little ESP from time to time. Listen to these signals, because they are usually right.

PRINCIPLES OF SUCCESSFUL MANAGEMENT

Business analysts Thomas J. Peters and Frank H. Waterman, Jr., have observed and studied hundreds of successful companies and have concluded that much of the world's conventional wisdom on how to succeed in business is not valid. These two Stanford graduates have found the traditional approach to business isn't enough to ensure success. And not only that, they also argue that certain small businesses can succeed where large corporations fail. Devising grand plans where everything is closely analyzed often is self-defeating and a waste of time. In their book, *In Search of Excellence*, they list eight keys to success in business.

1. *Begin with a bias toward action.* The best companies encourage action over procrastination or extensive analysis.
2. *Stay close to the customer.* The best companies cultivate their customers, are fanatics about quality control, and use customer suggestions for product improvement and innovation.
3. *Encourage autonomy and entrepreneurship.* At the most successful companies, all employees are encouraged to practice creativity and practical risk-taking during the execution of their jobs.
4. *Understand that people are responsible for productivity.* Rank-and-file-employees are treated as adults; they are viewed as coequals by management.
5. *Encourage "hands-on" innovative values.* Winning companies have strong cultures. Values are maintained by personal and enthusiastic attention from top management.
6. *Stick to the knitting.* The best companies know the ins and outs and unique qualities of their particular business and don't diversify into unfamiliar fields.
7. *Keep the forms simple and the staffs lean.* Top staffs are kept small. The structures and organizations of the companies are kept simple and flexible.
8. *Employ "simultaneous loose-tight properties."* The best companies maintain a paradoxical combination of centralized and decentralized properties in their organizational structures. They are tight about the things that are truly important and extremely loose about the rest.

POWER THROUGH PEOPLE

Increasing your net worth to a huge sum is a terrific reward, but people are really the only thing that matter in this life. You will find that the rewards of building people into giants and letting them be themselves will give you a great feeling of contentment and peace of mind. The money is great, but those feelings are greater. If I had to choose between the wealth that I have accumulated and the feelings from friends, most of whom are close business associates and employees, it would not be a hard decision to make. There really is power through people in finances, and, more important, a sense of contribution to the world.

13

BE YOUR OWN PR AGENT

No one understands what you want to accomplish better than you do. No one can promote and cite your activities toward reaching your goal better than you can. Learning to do your own public relations well is an important part of clearing your path to success. Good self-PR alerts others where and how you're going. They'll step aside. They'll cheer you on.

At age fifteen, Brad Smithers, of Little Rock, Arkansas, made his first offer on a small house. At age sixteen, he acquired a piece of property, and at the ripe old age of eighteen he had acquired three rental properties and turned a $2000 investment into a $25,000 net worth in just two years. But he didn't stop there. His success expanded when the *Arkansas Gazette* printed a sizable article on young Smithers and his miniature financial empire. From that article, he immediately received offers from two different people asking him to take a total of $20,000 of their money to invest for them.

Brad's story indicates just one way among many that a public relations campaign can help you reach your financial goals. For example, if you have trouble borrowing money from banks when you need it, the right kind of press, even if it appeared a year or two before, can be very helpful in convincing the banker to give you the loan. It is far more effective for you to present the banker with a file of newspaper clippings about how great you are than it is for you to sit in his office and tell him the same thing. The clippings appear to be absolute fact without any hype, while the self-sell almost always seems inflated.

Most large US corporations spend hundreds of thousands of dollars on PR to present an image of their company or product that will have long-lasting, positive effects in the minds of consumers, creditors, bankers, and the general public. You can do the same thing. The benefits are not only large, but last for many, many years, sometimes much longer than you would think possible.

CREDIBILITY IN PRINT

Properly planned PR can put you on the front page of the newspapers and give you instant credibility.

The fact that you wrote the newspaper articles yourself and said wonderful things about yourself is unknown once the article is in print. If it were known, no doubt people would be turned off. What I am saying is that: (1) You can quickly build your own credibility if you get the right stories in the media about yourself. Then it appears that someone else is tooting your horn. (2) You actually can promote those stories yourself and make sure that the right things get said.

The following article, reprinted from *The Indianapolis News* of March 29, 1982, might strike you as being a little self-serving for me, but it served Dick Hamilton well. When he sent me the clipping it was accompanied by the note: "Mark, your system works. This release was printed *exactly* as I submitted it."

HOUSING LIGHTS HIS FIRE

By ROBERT CORYA

Dick Hamilton is a self-described tycoon, coming on like a lottery winner who forgot he entered, a fellow confronting a malfunctioning candy machine as it dumps its entire load for a quarter.

Hamilton is a 40-year-old Tech High School graduate caught up in a frenzy of real estate dealings.

He's intent on sharing his newfound bonanza.

Seven years ago he started Wholesale Lighting Service at 500 N. Dearborn. Twenty months ago he sought some kind of tax shelter for that company. The tax toll was substantial.

He didn't have large sums of money, and in fact he believes a $10 paperback was really the sum and substance of his story.

The book is "Financial Genius" by Mark O. Haroldsen, a big seller since it appeared in 1976 under the title "How to Wake Up the Financial Genius in You" and since its revision in 1980.

Hamilton confirms it woke him up but big.

Here's his story. Income-producing real estate—houses, doubles, apartments—seemed the way to go. He liked what could be bought with little down from sellers in a hurry for whatever reasons.

Hamilton calls income-producing real estate a "forgiving investment," that is, if a purchase appears to have been a bad one, inflation, value appreciation, cash flow and tax advantages seem to turn the "bads" into the "goods."

He insists such investments "are safer than beginning investors realize."

One of his first purchases was a 49-unit apartment building downtown, with 32 units vacant, and had been several years. The out-of-state older owner had the apartments built 60 years earlier. Hamilton bought it with money borrowed against the Hamilton residence where he lives with his wife and two young daughters. That gave him the downpayment, and a contract was arranged for the balance.

A Quick Fixup

His first priority was to fix the place, painting, plastering, carpeting. In short order, he says, the vacant 32 units were filled.

The guidelines for the transaction came, in the main, from "Financial Genius." And he learned by doing, he said.

With that first acquisition completed, Hamilton and his wife attended real estate seminars (tax-deductible) around the United States and Europe, learning more at every turn.

In the 20 months since that first venture, Hamilton has acquired another apartment with 24 units, also downtown, and several doubles about town—92 units in all, valued at about $500,000.

Some were bought with nothing down; some with small amounts down. All the deals 100 percent legitimate and to the satisfaction of buyer and sellers.

The News and The Star classifieds, he said, are ideal places to search for the kinds of properties he wants. He also favors talking with real estate agents knowledgeable in income and investment property.

Persons who own income-producing real estate are usually willing to share the how-to, Hamilton says.

Finding "motivated sellers" is a key element to success, he says. These might be older people moving out-of-state, divorced people, someone tired of being the landlord for property and tenants.

Property needing fixing up appeals to him because he says that after some paint and cleaning, the cost of the maintenance is usually far less than the increased value.

Future Looks Good

Hamilton says all factors in such deals are negotiable—price, downpayment, interest rates. No real estate deal is a win-lose proposition, he said. It's a win-win situation—the seller wins, the buyer wins, the tenants win (although he acknowledged he has raised some low-rent units considerably, but only because they had been low for the last 30 years or more, in one case 60 years).

He is optimistic about the Indianapolis market in the months ahead.

Now, after these past 20 months, Hamilton agrees his lighting-fixture company became the dog that was wagged by his tax-sheltering tail. The latter is doing almost better than the former.

THE PRINTED WORD IS HOLY

Most people think something in print is a lot holier than the spoken word, so get in print. The first step in getting your story in a newspaper or a magazine or on TV or radio is simple. Ask. But you must know whom to ask and how to ask. Probably the easiest "whom" is the small weekly newspaper. These newspapers usually go begging for news, and they love to have human interest stories. It is particularly easy to get them to accept your material if the story is already laid out for them and is in a newspaper or newstype form. I've seen stories written by people that have been reprinted exactly as they were turned in, without one single word being changed.

If you really want your story or some PR about you in print in a hurry, send out your news release to every weekly newspaper within five hundred miles of where you live. You will find that it is easier to get your story run in an out-of-town paper because an out-of-towner has more of a mystique than a local boy.

Though weekly newspapers are a good place to start, don't eliminate the daily papers, even the larger ones. When dealing with larger publications you need a unique approach because the larger papers are bombarded with news releases and they must decide which to run and which not to.

OBLIGATE THE PRESS

One approach that is very effective in breaking into larger newspapers is to contact a columnist. Years ago, my father, who was a long-time newspaperman, advised me that if I helped reporters to gather information, they would return the favor by writing a story about me. A columnist can write a column about you or about any one of a thousand people very similar to you. So in order to get him to write about *you*, you must sit down and talk with him and show him why he should choose you. A lunch or dinner is in order. Tell him about your field of expertise or what you are doing that seems to be newsworthy. If your information makes his job easier, he will feel obligated to mention you in a column or do a story about you at that time or at some future time.

Most people don't take the time to do this kind of thing either because they are not aware that it can be done, or because they are too timid, or because they don't want to expend the energy. There is of course a point at which wooing a columnist is premature: do something newsworthy first.

GRAB THE HEADLINES

How does one grab the headlines? That's a tough one. The simple way is by being different. Short of a criminal act, how can you end up on the front page of the newspapers or magazines? You can be an extraordinary person or have the most fascinating story and still not make it to the front page. People who are cover stories for *Time* magazine or other big publications are usually people who have accomplished a lot. With few exceptions, they must make it happen. (See more on making it happen in Chapter 2.)

Thinking is the first essential ingredient in grabbing headlines. Sitting down and thinking something through can be worth a fortune to you. Think of a unique twist to an old idea; relate the normally unrelated. (See Chapter 5 for more on this.) Observe what is hot right now, what is being talked about, and capitalize on that. For example, when the government decided to sell quantities of its land, and everybody was talking about it, I volunteered my services as a host to a Houston network TV station to speak to their audience on the subject. The topic was hot and they wanted someone to talk about it, and they couldn't seem to find anybody who was an expert on the subject. I told them that I had written a book on real estate investing, and that got me on the show. What I didn't tell them was that I was not an expert by any stretch of the imagination on large tracts of land for development, nor did I at the time know much about the government-owned land. As soon as they agreed to have me as a guest, you better believe I quickly found out all I could on the big land sales. I got exposure in the Houston area and they got answers to the questions they wanted, and everyone was happy. I capitalized on what was happening right then. You can do the same thing with a little bit of thought and a lot of follow-through—contacts by letter or phone, or both.

Some people are always in the news. Their names are always popping up. So the average man on the street thinks they are much more brilliant than themselves and have accomplished much more. But more frequently the case is that they are the ones who are thinking of ways to capitalize on what is going on currently and they have established themselves by asking to appear on radio and talk shows and in newspaper and magazine articles. Remember: the results from such exposure can be phenomenal—and long-lasting. It is well worth your time to pursue publicity. Even though you will have some fears as you blunder ahead, remember the IGDS philosophy and keep in mind that the world will step aside for you if you know where you are going.

IT'S TRUE ABOUT THE "RIGHT" PEOPLE

The old saw "It's not what you know but who you know" has some truth. The problem is, most people assume that if they were not born at the right social level, complete with the right contacts from family and friends from birth, they are automatically going to be left out.

The good news is that anyone can have the right contacts if he or she takes the time to develop those contacts. The time that it takes is not nearly as much as most would guess. And there is no question about it, the right person at the right time saying the right thing to the right people can quickly put you on financial easy street. Make the contacts and then follow through.

KEY CONTACTS AND FAVORS

A major hurdle is that most people are too shortsighted. They don't see the long-term effects of key contacts and favors owed them. From a long-range point of view, you can be more patient in your actions and your thoughts. The long-term effect of special things that you have done for friends, for business acquaintances, and for contacts, is phenomenal.

Words may give an impression, but action and gestures make a much bigger impression. Can you think of special things acquaintances have done for you? I will never forget as long as I live being interrupted during a tennis tournament match by a man dressed in a ridiculous outfit who pranced onto the court to deliver a singing telegram. The message was from someone I had stood up for an appointment. Even though the telegram disrupted the match, I knew it was done all in good fun, and it made a lasting impression. (By the way, my opponent apparently couldn't handle the shock, and I went on to win the match.) I can think of very unusual gifts from people I least expected them from at very unexpected times. Gifts and gestures of this kind make big impressions on my mind; I have never forgotten the deeds or the doers.

As you plan your financial life, take time to develop the right contacts by doing unusual good deeds for those who can help you. Keep in mind that you are in it for the long haul. These people won't forget you when you need them to do things for you.

EIGHT WORDS FROM THE RIGHT PERSON AT THE RIGHT TIME

Bankers, brokers, politicians, city commissioners, judges, attorneys, presidents of corporations, and other people in your community and state can be of invaluable service.

The eight words that can mean the difference between success and failure in any given event are: "Would you please help my friend John Smith?" If your name is John Smith, and you need a loan from a bank, and the president of that bank calls his key loan officer and says those eight words, the likelihood of your getting a loan is very high.

But obviously the first step is that you need to get to know the president of the bank, and that's really not that hard to do. So the question becomes, how can you get to know them? What are some easy steps you can take to make the right contacts?

MAKING CONTACTS

Number 1: Make two lists, one of people you want to get to know and the other of people whom you have made initial contact with and are starting to get to know. The key here is to keep excellent records with the person's name, address and phone number, the name of his secretary, his wife, his children and their interests, hobbies, pastimes, and passions. Every time you call or write or have contact with them, you can use this information to cement your relationship.

Number 2: Write lots of letters. Start to take pride in the list of people you know, then do things for them. Send them items or information that will help them. For example, the bank president I do the most business with is invited to all my important social functions and we play tennis regularly. I always let him win. (Of course he's the better player anyway!) He likes my business and is always doing nice things back.

Number 3: Have the guts to add action to your thoughts. That means, if you think you want to meet the mayor, the governor, a senator, or the president of almost any organization, go do it. Make the necessary phone calls and the visits to the office. Even camp out in his or her waiting room, if necessary, thus letting the receptionist know that you are not leaving until you see Mr. or Ms. Big.

Number 4: Use the "friend-of-a-friend" approach. David Rockefeller, the chairman of the board of the Chase Manhattan Bank, has a list of influential people around the world that is kept on a computer. These lists can be printed out alphabetically by city, state, country, and occupation—banker, lawyer, politician, etc.

It's a fantastic system. Just think of it. When David Rockefeller visits Singapore, all he has to do is to ask his secretary to push the right button to get a list of all the political, social, or banking contacts he wants to make there. Ditto for Chicago, San Francisco, Hong Kong, or London. You can have the same kind of system on a smaller basis in your own town, city, or state.

One of the easiest ways to build a large name-file is by using the friend-of-a-friend concept. Think about how many friends you have. Even if you only have five friends and you call each one of them and ask if he or she has five other influential or semi-influential people whom you can call and get to know or invite to a party or whatever, I am sure that each of your five friends could give you five more names. If you make contact with each of these referrals, it will jump your contacts from five to thirty—five original friends, plus the other twenty-five. If you ask each of those twenty-five for five of their friends' names for contacts, that would jump your total contacts to 155 people. One more step on this geometric progression would be a total of 780 contacts. As you can see, in a very short time you can build quite a large system with more people than you can get to know. The important thing is to focus on those contacts who will help you the most in the long run. Get them in your debt and then collect over time to enhance both your financial lives.

FAKE-IT-TILL-YOU-MAKE-IT SYNDROME

The "fake-it-till-you-make-it" syndrome works if you do. If you don't, the fake remains fake and unfulfilled. If your vivid imaginings of your goal are backed by dogged determination and effort, then those qualities, dreams, and goals and your "faking" quickly begin to be realities.

If you are working your tail off, your actions validate and give credibility to your work. People will believe you and begin to applaud your success even when you are a long way from it. (The nice thing about this is that their applause will motivate you all the more.)

The plastic façade effected by phonies is quite a different thing from the sincere, hardworking entrepreneur who visualizes his success and lives as if he had already achieved it. The phony is stagnant and will remain phony. That is the fulfillment of his or her "loss of self-prophecy," since any reality seeps out. On the other hand, the courageous achiever's dynamism radiates with the energy that is turning dreams into realities. Others can be taken in only briefly by plastic façades of wealth, façade actions, and empty talk, talk, talk. Realistic action toward financial goals works; talk doesn't.

Recently, I was in Acapulco playing tennis with a friend. As we sat near the pool after an exhausting match, talking about what we wanted to accomplish, Paul Meyer told me that he would send me a document that would be helpful to me. Pulling an oversized wallet from his pocket, he asked me if I had been receiving what he had promised at our various meetings to send me. I assured him that everything he had promised to send had arrived. This included everything from cassette tapes to books, from copies of contracts to special testing forms. At that point Paul said, "I'll bet you've never met anyone with better follow-through than me." I told him that I hadn't.

I had always admired his remarkable follow-through. I thought about how wonderful the business world, or the world in general, would be if everyone followed through on every promise. I made some resolves that day that have been tremendously rewarding. Then later I realized that when Paul boasted that his follow-through was the best, he at that very moment was forcing himself into a corner (which he wished to do) to insure that he would continue to be the best. He was doing a little "faking" so as to improve his "making."

I realized that many people's failure to follow through on what they say is not intentional, but more the result of inefficiency and lapse of memory.

Paul's system ensures follow-through. It is very simple. He

people lose money when somebody is very persuasive and convinces them that it is a "can't lose" situation with huge profits available. If it really is that green, then get into it, but get into it with control over processes and outcome.

Control is critical because no one cares about someone else's money as much as he does about his own. *If you invest in other people's ventures, keep control of the money.* This is a simple but extremely vital point to avoid a common financial bear trap. Remember: many people can tell good stories, but they usually are better talkers than doers.

If you invest in such ventures, you must take a huge amount of time to check them out thoroughly. And I mean really investigate. You need to be a super skeptic and take nothing for granted. I don't care if the person presenting the deal to you is a close friend or relative. They still need to be checked out.

MAKE CONTROL YOUR POLICY

We will usually take no for an answer when an institution or company tells us that what we have asked for is against policy. We should learn something from that. *Individuals, like institutions, should set policies and stick to those policies in most cases.* If somebody asks you to invest in his deal, you can easily get out of it by saying, "Sorry, I have a policy against doing that." Say it very matter-of-factly and very firmly. By doing this, you have eliminated the hassle and the long sales pitch that you usually get.

THE PRETTIER THE PACKAGE, THE CRUMMIER THE DEAL

A number of years ago, before I made the policy of not investing in other people's deals unless I had control, I put a total of several hundred thousand dollars into five different ventures. All but one were tax-shelter deals. There was a coal-mine deal in West Virginia, an oil tax-shelter, a recreational-land deal, a videotape deal, and I even financed a movie. Since I had sold tax shelters earlier when I was a stockbroker, I should have realized how unwise I was to put my money where I didn't have control. In examining the deal after the fact (in this case I was as dumb as the average guy, who always does his heaviest research and the most detailed checking after he has already bought), I noticed that the deals that were in fancy packages as thick as phone books, complete with pictures and nice graphics, beautiful covers with the most glowing opinions from attorneys and CPAs, were the crummiest of all.

Ever since that observation, I have done some unscientific research and discovered how many pre-packed deals seem to support this conclusion. The deals from which I have made the most money were not packaged with all the whistles and bells. I conclude that if someone has taken the time, money, and energy to put the package into an almost perfect form, with all of the above-mentioned items, most of the financial benefits have already been taken out of it by those same people.

In the case of the five investments mentioned above, the ones that were tax shelters were challenged by the IRS and we lost. I ended up paying a lot of back taxes because of that. The ones that weren't tax shelters were absolute busts. As a matter of fact, I lost every single dollar that I put in every single one of those ventures.

I realize that my experience is not necessarily universal. Certainly, not every single venture you don't control turns sour. But I am saying that from my experience, the lion's share of them are worthless or will turn out to be such. *If you want to increase your odds of keeping what you have made and making more from that, stay away from other people's deals.* Put your money in your own deals. The only exceptions I would make to this are in the ventures where you know and thoroughly trust the other parties. Not only do you have to trust the person and his integrity, but also his judgment. Read more on this subject under "Trusting Versus Skepticism" in this chapter.

LAWSUITS ARE FOR DUMMIES
NOT DOERS

If you want to accomplish things and you are a person who gets things done, stay away from lawsuits. They are counter-productive and expensive. They will waste your time, your money, and, most of all, your mental energy. Sure, there are times when suing is the only thing you can do. And there are times when somebody else will sue you. But settle whenever you can. I am not saying you should settle a lawsuit by paying something that you don't owe. I don't believe in legalized blackmail, and unfortunately many lawsuits are just that. In an honest dispute, when compromise on both sides can avoid a lawsuit, compromise. You will be saving much more than time and money. When you lock horns in a fight, that fight can begin to dominate your thoughts and concerns, distracting you from more important, productive matters.

Try to talk to the person who has filed the suit against you before filing a countersuit. I mean, face to face. Try to resolve your differences as adults. Two people who are fair and honest can almost always settle their disputes. After all, they will always know more about the dispute than the judge. In full-blown litigation it takes three or four days for the judge just to understand what the dispute is all about. This financial trap grabs many people because their egos get in the way. If you can back off and observe yourself and take a look at the entire situation, you can avoid it.

ASK YOUR BARBER HOW TO CUT HAIR, NOT HOW TO MAKE MONEY

It is amazing how many people seek or listen to financial advice from neighbors who are in approximately the same financial position as themselves. Others run to their bankers to ask if a particular deal is any good or not. What do bankers know about deals? Zip. Sure, a banker knows about loans and checking accounts, and he or she knows a lot about accounting, and borrowing and relending money, because that is bank business. Deals are not. Since people know that there is money in banks, they tend to think that the bankers know how to earn it. Remember, they are just custodians, they are just janitors of money. It's not their own money, it's yours.

Barbers work on heads, but that doesn't make them psychologists, because they work only on the outside of the head, not the inside, so their psychological advice or how-to-make-money advice is not very credible. Avoid this trap by doing some of your own thinking.

The best place to go to learn how to make money is to somebody who has made a lot of it. What better place to go than to an entrepreneur who started from scratch and did it all himself? I wouldn't even want to approach someone like David Rockefeller. Sure, he has several hundred million dollars and he is the chairman of the board of one of the largest banks in the world, but his grandfather, John D. Rockefeller, is the one who made the big bucks. Ever since then, David and his brothers have just been keeping track of it. Sure, they made it grow. But if I am starting out and have yet to make my first million, I need to talk to somebody who has been in the same shoes I'm in.

DEAL BREAKERS VERSUS DEAL MAKERS

Everybody needs advisers, but the advisers you need to surround yourself with should be deal makers, not breakers. Sure, you and only you should be the one making the final decisions, but I find that all of us can be influenced and helped by smart people whose opinions we hold in high regard.

Generally speaking, I find from experience that attorneys are deal breakers, not deal makers. Knowing that, I usually structure the whole deal before I have an attorney get involved at all. Yes, I want him or her involved. When? Just before I sign the papers. I want him to read the contract to make sure everything is legal. I want to know I have covered all the legal bases. That is what he learned to do in his schooling and that is what he is best at. Problems arise when he steps into a management role. In defense of him, it must be said that he is paid to keep you out of trouble, so most of the time he will have a negative outlook on whatever you are doing. When going to an attorney for legal advice, you should always be sure that you ask very precise questions and not let him overstep his bounds. He will if you let him. He has to play the devil's advocate, and that is good, but don't let him unduly influence you. The same applies to your CPA, your business managers, and your bankers.

Bankers are a lot like attorneys in that they have to look at things from a defensive point of view. Before they make a loan they always have to see what could happen under the worst possible conditions. They must always consider how they are going to get their money back if you default. I would take the same stance if I were lending money. But these people can't make your decisions. Only you can. So listen to their advice, knowing that you are going to get some negative advice and that many times you are going to have to override it. Remember: that is the real separator. You have to supply the guts. You have to give the courage. You have to decide to make it happen, risk or not.

COMMON SENSE IS UNSOPHISTICATED

One definition of common sense is "what is sound and prudent but often unsophisticated." I've seen many very sophisticated business decisions that have lost millions of dollars. To avoid financial traps, you need a huge dose of common sense, especially when those all around you are playing sophisticated and getting wrapped up with what is hot or in vogue.

DO NOTHING AND MAKE 250% RETURN

Common sense will keep you from being trapped or pushed or bullied or shocked into doing a deal that you don't want to do. An insistent, fast-talking, logical person many times can persuade somebody to do something he doesn't really want to do. If somebody asked you if you would like a 250% return without risk and without effort, they wouldn't be coming to you to borrow your money. If a deal were really that good, the promoters would have no trouble getting the needed money from a bank or banks. The simple fact is, those kinds of returns don't consistently exist. Not at least without effort. Deals like that don't come all packaged neat and nice, especially with the claim that it is riskless. Believe me, it won't happen! If I had a return like that without any effort or risk, you'd better believe that I would be able to borrow a whole lot of money at 20% to take advantage of the 230% return. *Common sense is recognizing reality and then acting accordingly.*

HOW TO STOP THEM FROM CONTROLLING YOU

You must realize first of all what is happening when someone is trying to manipulate you. Identifying what is happening will keep it from happening. If you have taken time beforehand to pre-think your response to manipulative questions and have standard answers on the tip of your tongue to counteract such questions, you will be able to sidestep or flatly turn down this kind of approach with ease. And if words don't do the trick (such as "No, I have made it a policy never to invest any of my money where I don't have absolute control"), then you need to take action. Many people will not be deterred by what you say. But virtually everyone will respond to firm and quick action.

By using past events, people are manipulated all the time. They fall into the second-thought, "you-should-have," trap. You hear that all the time, not only about your day-to-day behavior with your friends and relatives and loved ones but also in the investment world: "You should have bought this," and, "You should have done that." But the fact of the matter is you can't change what you should have done. Time has already passed; the past is over: there is nothing that you can do about that. So you shouldn't let anybody manipulate or victimize you by using that kind of so-called logic. Be alert to other reproaches or appeals that are victimizing. We hear them every day. People say:

- Why did you do it that way?
- If only you had consulted me first.
- But we've always done it this way.
- If you said it before, why don't you mean it now?
- If only I hadn't done that.
- Why, just yesterday we had an example similar to yours.
- Whose fault was it?

Recognize these statements for what they are, and take appropriate action. Don't be victimized.

In order to get attention from some people we need to put action where our mouth is. Sometimes words, words, words just do not convey the message. If you realize somebody is trying to manipulate you into doing something you don't want, react with some surprise unexpected action and you will get their attention.

TRUSTING VERSUS SKEPTICISM

I know a few individuals I would trust completely. In fact, I'd give them $100,000 cash tomorrow and say, hold on to this cash for me for a few days, I'll be back for it. And I would know without any doubt that it would be safe with them. Unfortunately, I know very few people like this and it took quite a while to develop that kind of trust.

I am appalled by people who will invest their life savings with a person they have just met and known only a few months. Sure, sometimes this new "trusted friend" seems to be trustworthy, but he really hasn't proven himself. Safety comes in the proof. I have some simple rules that I now follow which seem to protect me in all cases. These are my policies:

- It's okay to trust and trust fully, but a person must earn the trust, and that takes time.
- I observe very carefully what a person does and give it ten times more weight than what he or she says. It's easy to say that you are great, honest, smart, etc., but both liars and honest men say the same thing. I also look to see if their deeds correlate closely with what they say.
- In trusting someone I separate his honesty from his judgment. I know many people whom I trust implicitly, but I question their judgment. People like this can be used by others. If they are convinced by some smooth-talking salesman that a particular investment is good when they tell you about it, they are being totally honest, for they believe that what they are saying is the truth. So I may trust their words because of prior proof, but I may also challenge their judgment.
- I am always a super skeptic at first. I always question the other person's motive. Why should he tell me about this great once-in-a-lifetime deal just because he likes me? I'm sorry, I don't buy that line. Every time someone has told me he is doing something only for me, and that there is nothing in it for him, I've lost. Human nature is just not that way. Business relationships as well as personal relationships have to have something in it for both parties or somebody gets hurt.

15

TAX BENEFITS OF REAL ESTATE: HOW TO CUT YOUR TAXES TO ZERO

When I first started in real estate I knew very little about income tax. For me, real estate represented a way to reach a goal; a way to unleash the financial genius inside me and a way to become very wealthy in a short period of time. I achieved all of these goals, and in the process I learned of all the tax benefits that ownership of real estate can give. These tax benefits were the icing on the cake.

Later, after having become involved in scores of deals, I more fully appreciated the breadth and depth of all the tax benefits available. The use of these income tax benefits is not a loophole, but merely a response to the laws of Congress. These laws have arisen from Congress's perception of the housing needs of the country, and Congress's apparent conclusion that the housing stock of this country is too important to be left to HUD.

After I learned the secrets of becoming wealthy through real estate, I wanted to share this knowledge with others and I began giving seminars. I was fortunate to be associated with Dick Lee, the country's top expert in the income tax aspects of real property ownership. Dick and I have shared many long discussions at our in-depth, week-long seminars and at my headquarters in Salt Lake City. Dick's philosophy is much like mine. We both have three rules regarding any investment:

1. Is it safe—will I get my money back?
2. Is it profitable—will I make money?

Only if we can answer yes to questions one and two do we ask:

3. Are there tax benefits?

Once that I am convinced that I have a winner, the tax benefits make a sweet deal a lot sweeter.

Some of the tax benefits I look for in a real estate deal are:

- Positive cash flow with zero tax
- Tax-free refinancing
- 20% lid on capital-gains taxes, or
- Indefinite deferment of tax by exchanging

We will talk about these things and much more in this chapter.

If you had to pay $7982 cash out of your pocket next April 15, I am sure that you would do a lot more looking into ways to cut that tax bill than you do now. Since most people have their income taxes slowly deducted from their paychecks, they are able to digest it more easily. Consequently, they don't try very hard to figure ways to reduce or cut their tax bill to zero. And that's too bad, because it is not that hard to zero out on your taxes.

HOW TO GIVE YOURSELF A $7982 RAISE THIS YEAR

You can give yourself a $7982 raise this year without making any more money. You do it by merely not paying income tax. Of course, you must do it legally or you will end up in a small, one-bedroom, poorly furnished apartment complete with bars on the windows. Seventy-nine hundred and eighty-two dollars is the federal tax you will pay if you have a taxable income of $32,000. With the inflation we have had the past years, there are a lot of people making a lot more than that paying much bigger tax bills. Incidentally, if you had made that same $32,000 in 1913, your tax bill would have been a whopping $140—the income tax law was put on the books as a "temporary" measure to solve the government's financial problems. Their definition of temporary is different from the one in my dictionary.

Cutting your taxes by almost $8000 is much easier than you think. Most people think only the rich can cut their taxes to zero. Not so. In fact, with the tax law changes made in the Economic Recovery Tax Act of 1981, it's much easier to zero out your taxes.

KEY #1: THE MILLION-DOLLAR WORD "DEPRECIATION"

The single most important key to tax benefits for real estate owners is depreciation. The Tax Act of 1981 made some tremendous improvements in the tax benefits given to us by depreciation (they even gave it a new name—Accelerated Cost Recovery System—but everybody still calls it depreciation just the same). When you fill out your income tax forms, in the part of the return that relates to your income property you state first the income from the property and then all of your cash expenses, for interest, taxes, utilities, repairs, and so on. But in addition to these out-of-the-pocket expenses, you can also deduct depreciation.

ACRS, or depreciation, doesn't mean the opposite of appreciation. That's where most people get confused. The tax word "depreciation" is a term that doesn't necessarily have anything to do with the real world. Depreciation is something that you get to deduct from your taxable income that doesn't cost you anything. It is only a paper loss. In the real world there was no loss at all. In fact, there can be a big gain and you can still deduct depreciation or ACRS. Depreciation is a charge for the wearing out of your building, and is allowed by the IRS as a cost of doing business. It doesn't matter if the value of a building is actually appreciating. You can still write off depreciation and turn what may have been a modest cash profit into a loss for income tax purposes. And you can use that loss to offset other income, say W-2 income. That is how real estate can lead to lower income taxes and possibly zero income taxes. I know, because I zeroed out a good number of times in my earlier years and both Dick Lee and I get letters every year from seminar attendees who have done the same.

CAPITAL OR EXPENSE?

Before discussing how the new depreciation works, let's think a minute about whether we should depreciate at all. It's clear that many expenses do not need to be depreciated at all and can be written off in full in the year incurred; the problem is deciding which is which. After reading the tax books we have come up with some ground rules. In plumbing, for instance, leaky-faucet repairs are deductible as an expense. If the hot-

and cold-water piping has to be completely replaced with copper, that would have to be depreciated. However, if a disposal or two are installed, these are written off as expenses, since the building is being put back where it was, but its life not increased appreciably. Any painting done is deducted even if I paint the whole building exterior, since that does not increase the useful life of the building. If I put in a few pieces of furniture or an appliance or two to replace what was already there, I would expense these items. But if I decided to change from unfurnished to furnished and put in several thousand dollars' worth of furniture, I would depreciate this investment, using the ACRS five-year life.

DEPRECIATION

There really aren't that many choices to be made in ACRS: it's a mink-lined straitjacket. There are four choices of depreciation for buildings: (1) forty-five-year straight line, (2) thirty-five-year straight line, and (3) fifteen-year ACRS. I use (4) the fifteen-year straight line almost exclusively if I can't use the extra depreciation benefits of accelerated. Similarly, while I can select other "lives," I expect to use a five-year life only for furnishings and appliances and a three-year life for cars. So for me, ACRS means three things to remember: Buildings are fifteen-year ACRS, cars are three-year ACRS, and everything else is five-year ACRS. "Everything else" includes items such as furniture, furnishings, appliances, and a computer if I can use it in my rental business. But not major components, like the building, which must be fifteen-year ACRS.

Under ACRS you are allowed to deduct a percentage of the item's cost over each year of the recovery period. Table 3 gives percentages for the most common items.

ACRS applies only to the building and not to the land.

You are no longer required to allocate the purchase price between land and building according to the property-tax bill (though the IRS will generally go along with that). If I feel that my building represents a larger portion of my purchase price, and I can substantiate this with an appraisal (not too hard to do and costing only a few hundred dollars), I will calculate ACRS using this larger amount.

So much for the nuts and bolts of depreciation. What are the benefits? What's the bottom line? Let's compare the old method (twenty-year straight line) with the new (fifteen-year

Table 3

PERCENTAGE OF RECOVERY

Year	Car	Furniture Furnishings Appliances Computer	Building or Major Component*
1	25%	15%	12%
2	38	22	10
3	33	21	9
4		21	8
5		21	7
6			6
7			6
8			6
9			6
10			5
11			5
12			5
13			5
14			5
15			5

* If purchased in January.

ACRS). The building was bought in January for a total cost of $800,000 and a building-to-land ratio of 80%, leaving $640,000 for the building. Here are the comparisons for the first three years:

Year	Old Law	ACRS	Difference
1	$32,000	$ 76,800*	$ 44,800
2	32,000	64,000	32,000
3	32,000	57,600	25,600
	$96,000	$198,400	$102,400

* This figure was arrived at by using Table 4. The first year ACRS is 12% on 12% × $640,000 = $76,800.

This is a dramatic increase in depreciation: 140% the first year, 100% the second, and 80% the third, for an average increase of over 100% for the three years.

What will this mean to you in your income tax return? Assuming typical income and expense figures it would look like this:

	Old Style	ACRS
Income	$100,000	$100,000
Less expenses	90,000	90,000
Cash flow	$ 10,000	$ 10,000
Less depreciation	32,000	76,800
Net loss	$(22,000)	$(66,800)

If you wanted to zero out with about $60,000 of other income, it would have taken three buildings under the old style, but only one with ACRS.

ACRS VERSUS S/L

Is there a time when you shouldn't use the Accelerated Cost Recovery System and instead should use the straight-line cost recovery? Generally, I use Accelerated Cost for residential buildings and straight-line cost for commercial or industrial buildings or shopping centers.

I won't go into detail, but if you have bought a nonresidential building and are thinking of using ACRS, I most strongly recommend that you consult with an experienced tax preparer before doing so, for if you use ACRS, all of your gain stemming from the depreciation will be fully taxable as ordinary income and will not get the capital-gain treatment (see Key #5).

KEY #2: TAX PLANNING

Key #2 is tax planning. You can't plan very well on the last days, week, or month of the year. It's usually too late. Though there are a few things you can do at the last moment, your options start to be limited drastically. I've noticed a great proliferation of tax-shelter deals that are less than reputable being sold in this last month. The sellers and promoters of such tax shelters know that you don't have a lot of time to check them out, nor do you have a lot of options. So start thinking now about next year and making appropriate plans to purchase the appropriate assets that give you maximum write-offs.

If you use ACRS, but wait till December to purchase property, you have lost most of the benefits for that particular year. For example, if you were to buy an apartment building or rental house in the tenth month of the year, you would be allowed to deduct only 3% of the purchase price (less the land value) in the year you bought it. But if the property were bought in the second month, you would be able to deduct 11% of the purchase price less the land value.

Table 4

ALL REAL ESTATE (Except Low-Income Housing)
The applicable percentage is:

(Use the column for the month in the first year
the property is placed in service)

Years	Month First Placed in Service											
	1	2	3	4	5	6	7	8	9	10	11	12
1	12%	11%	10%	9%	8%	7%	6%	5%	4%	3%	2%	1%
2	10	10	11	11	11	11	11	11	11	11	11	12
3	9	9	9	9	10	10	10	10	10	10	10	10
4	8	8	8	8	8	8	9	9	9	9	9	9
5	7	7	7	7	7	7	8	8	8	8	8	8
6	6	6	6	6	7	7	7	7	7	7	7	7
7	6	6	6	6	6	6	6	6	6	6	6	6
8	6	6	6	6	6	6	6	6	6	6	6	6
9	6	6	6	6	5	6	5	5	5	6	6	6
10	5	6	5	6	5	5	5	5	5	5	6	5
11	5	5	5	5	5	5	5	5	5	5	5	5
12	5	5	5	5	5	5	5	5	5	5	5	5
13	5	5	5	5	5	5	5	5	5	5	5	5
14	5	5	5	5	5	5	5	5	5	5	5	5
15	5	5	5	5	5	5	5	5	5	5	5	5
16	—	—	1	1	2	2	3	3	4	4	4	5

KEY #3: STRATEGY VERSUS DETAIL

Key #3 is knowing the overall strategy of what you want to do and understanding that strategy. Do not get carried away with details and spend time reading IRS bulletins and updates. Those details are better left with the professional, your CPA, to do. In your overall strategy, you should be figuring exactly how much property you need to buy to cut your taxes to zero. In your overall strategy meeting you can ask for the assistance of your CPA or tax adviser to make sure you get the numbers right. But once you have that plan, it's more important that you make sure the plan is executed.

KEY #4: PICK THE BEST TAX MAN

Key #4 ties closely into #3. Make sure that you hire the best CPA or tax man in your area. You need someone aggressive but impeccably honest; someone who will stay up-to-date on all the details but doesn't get so bogged down that he or she forgets the overall strategy. You might think that you are paying an enormous price when you get your accountant's bill. But by using someone who is not the best, you end up paying for them to learn as they go. I would rather pay a higher hourly rate and not pay for the man or woman's education. And besides, the fee is tax deductible.

It really is critical that you find a good tax man. A good tax man will: (1) steer you to maximum deductions, (2) inform you of deductions that you had no idea existed, (3) help you plan overall strategies to help you zero out, and (4) act as a middleman and negotiator if you are audited by the IRS.

The first time I ever had somebody else help me with my taxes, he told me that it would cost me a couple of hundred dollars. At that time the fee seemed enormous relative to my income, but he assured me he could save me at least $1000. (Keep in mind that this was after I had completely done my taxes for that year and thought that my anticipated refund would be as much as I could get out of them.) Upon his assurance I let him go ahead, and sure enough, my refund check was $1200 more than I figured it would be.

WHEN YOU SELL YOUR BUILDING

The Tax Code, which has allowed you to pay zero tax while you owned your building, while good to real estate investors, isn't perfect. If you sell your building you will almost certainly have to pay some tax on gain. These capital-gains taxes and two related areas, the recapture of excess depreciation and the possibility of a preference tax, are discussed next.

KEY #5: CAPITAL GAINS

The biggest break that real estate investors get at time of sale is that gains are taxed only to the extent of 40%; the other 60% is not subject to regular income tax.

Consider the following two tables:

Real-World Treatment

Sold for	$150,000
Bought for	75,000
"Real" Gain	$ 75,000

Tax Treatment

Sold for		$150,000
Bought for	75,000	
Less depreciation taken	25,000	50,000
"Tax" Gain		$100,000

These tables show that what the IRS giveth the IRS taketh away. The $25,000 of depreciation which the IRS lets you take in earlier years must now be added back in determining the gain so that your tax gain will always exceed the real gain by the amount of depreciation taken. But that's not really so bad, because the depreciation that you used in prior years and that you offset against ordinary income, was deductible to you at one hundred cents on the dollar. True enough, it has to be added back in and will increase the gain at sale, but the gain itself is taxed at only 40%. True enough, the depreciation has to be repaid, but only at forty cents on the dollar.

Since the tax gain of $100,000 is a capital gain (assuming the building was held for more than one year), the IRS lets you exclude $60,000. This is not subject to income tax. Only the remaining $40,000 is subject to income tax and is added into the rest of your taxable income. But since the maximum tax bracket is now 50%, that means that the most you can pay on a gain of $100,000 is $20,000 (50% × $40,000).

NET OPERATING LOSS

You have seen from the "net loss" table on page 188 how dramatically the paper losses from your building can increase by use of ACRS. In the example shown the loss jumped from $22,-000 to almost $67,000. With larger buildings, losses of $100,-000 or $200,000 or more are not unusual.

KEY #6: HOW TO RECEIVE THREE YEARS OF BACK TAXES

One of the benefits of the tax law is that losses like this can not only keep you from paying taxes in the current year, they can allow you to go back and get refunds for all of the taxes that you have paid for the prior three years!

That's right: you can actually go back, claim, and receive thousands of dollars that you have already paid, and the IRS will pay you interest on the time that they have "held" your money. This is done by the use of an amended return, Form 1040X. Many tax preparers overlook this tax-saving technique, which is completely approved by the IRS.

INCOME AVERAGING

It may turn out that by use of the ACRS method of depreciation that your taxable income will be zero for several years in a row, and then you may have a large taxable income owing perhaps to sale of a building. If this is so, the benefits of another tax technique, called *income averaging,* will be very useful to you.

Let's say you've sold a building and the gains were such that your taxable income jumps to $100,000. For a married person the tax on this would be over $37,000. But if you had zeroed out for the prior four years, your tax would drop to less than $15,000, a substantial savings! Income averaging will work just as well even if your prior years' taxable incomes were more than zero, of if the current year's taxable income is less than $100,000. All that's necessary is that the current year's taxable income exceeds 120% of the average of the prior four years by more than $3000. Your accountant should check this for you every year.

RECAPTURE OF EXCESS DEPRECIATION

Earlier, I said that I would generally always take Accelerated Cost Recovery rather than straight-line cost recovery. By taking Accelerated Cost, I could run into a problem at time of sale, but it is a small one. The IRS takes the position that if any part of that $25,000 worth of depreciation that I took in the example on page 191 was because of Accelerated Cost Recovery (namely, was in excess of the straight-line depreciation) then the part of my gain that was owing to the excess depreciation will be 100% ordinary income instead of 40% capital-gain income. This doesn't worry me, for two reasons. In the first place, the worst that could be said of recapture of excess depreciation is that I have to give back the IRS at one hundred cents on the dollar what I had previously deducted in prior years at one hundred cents on the dollar. If you think about it, this is really a pretty good break. I have had an interest-free loan from the government for up to several years. The other reason it doesn't trouble me is the amount of a typical gain where there is recapture of depreciation is very small—usually only 1% to 2% of the gain—and it is recaptured at straight line with all the rest getting the full capital-gains treatment.

PREFERENCE TAX

What about that 60% of the capital gain that I was allowed to deduct? Is that $60,000 completely free of income tax? The answer is probably yes. However, when you do have a capital gain, make sure that your tax preparer calculates whatever preference tax there may be, if any, and compares it with your regular income tax. If the preference tax is less than your regular income tax, as would usually be the case, you just ignore it. If the preference tax exceeds your regular income tax, you pay your regular income tax plus the difference. This subject is a complicated one, and is beyond the scope of this chapter. But if you plan to sell a building at any significant amount of gain, you really ought to check out the income tax aspects of the sale with a competent tax preparer even before you go into escrow.

INSTALLMENT SALES

Sometimes the person who is buying your building can't afford to pay cash down to a new loan and thus cash you out, and sometimes you would rather not have all cash but rather get your payment over a period of several years. In either event, if you take part of your profit back in the form of a note, you can elect to pay your tax on the installment-sale basis, a sort of pay-as-you-go plan. The calculations are complicated, but any competent tax preparer can help you with them. The thing to remember is that you don't have to pay your tax all at once in the year of sale (though you can if the circumstances are right and you prefer to). One thing I have learned: if you do take a note back you can of course elect the installment sale and pay the tax year by year as the note is paid off. However, if you use the note as, say, part of the downpayment on the purchase of another building, that will trigger the rest of the gain and the balance of the tax will have to be paid as of the year you use the note as downpayment. The same applies if you sell the note, of course, but there is a way around this. You can borrow against the note, using it as security. If you structure it right, the tax-deductible interest that you pay on your loan will balance out the taxable interest income from the note and you will have a good part of the cash now even though the tax is deferred until the note is paid off.

EXCHANGES

We just discussed the case in which an investor sold a building for $150,000. We found out that through various benefits in the Tax Code the tax on his or her capital gains should not be too distressing. A rule of thumb is that the tax on complete capital gains cash-out runs between 10% to 15% of the amount of the gain. In the case above, that means that the tax would be anywhere from $15,000 to $22,500. But what if you mean to use the proceeds from your sale to buy another building? You couldn't then buy as much of a building as you otherwise might have because of the $15,000 to $22,500, which has to be siphoned off to pay the IRS. If you plan to buy another building, what you should really think of is an exchange. In this case, Section 1031 of the IRS Code comes to the rescue. This section of the Code says essentially no gain or loss will be recognized if you exchange your building for another building rather than sell the first and buy the second. Certain rules apply: the mortgage you assume must be larger than the mortgage you give up, and you can't end up with any unlike property. Unlike property is anything that is not real estate; for instance, cash, notes, or other paper instruments; cars or what have you. It is not that difficult to do an exchange, though it is highly unlikely that it will be a two-way exchange, namely that you can find somebody with something you want and who wants your building. The usual exchange is a three-way exchange, though there can be many more legs in a complicated exchange.

In the usual three-way exchange you start the process by listing your building at a price and terms that you think are realistic, and when you find a buyer you simply stipulate that the buyer will cooperate in a Section 1031 exchange at no cost or obligation to him. I have never yet found a buyer who would not so agree. Let's say that your building will sell at $150,000, and that you owe $80,000, so that your equity is $70,000. Let's further say that the new buyer is going to put $30,000 down and will get a new loan for the balance. That means that if you actually sold the building you would get your $70,000 equity in cash. But you don't intend to sell the building because you don't want to pay that capital-gains tax. You have looked around for several weeks while the escrow was being finalized prior to its formal opening, and you have structured the deal so that you have a ninety-day escrow. Let's say that after about four or five weeks you find a building for $500,000 that otherwise fulfills your requirements. The only financing now on the building is a first mortgage for $320,000. In discussions with the seller or his or her agent you have found that he would probably agree to approximately $70,000 down and that he would carry back the balance of $110,000 in the form of a second mortgage. You then make your written offer to him, only instead of it being an offer for purchase on these terms, you offer to exchange your building for the downpayment. Otherwise the price and terms would be the same; you would assume his existing first mortgage and he would take back a second mortgage of $110,000. From a seller's standpoint, such an exchange is perfectly acceptable to him since your building is already in escrow.

The closing will be simultaneous though a little complicated. In Step 1, the seller will exchange his or her property for your property plus your assumption of the first mortgage and the new second mortgage. At this point you have successfully completed your exchange. In Step 2 of the escrow the purchase escrow occurs in that the buyer comes in with his or her $30,000 cash and new first-trust deed for $120,000, for a total of $150,000. The existing $80,000 first on your prior building is paid off, leaving $70,000, which goes to the down-trader. Everybody ends up where he wants to be. The initial buyer has bought his building for $150,000, according to his price and terms. The seller of the larger building has in effect sold his building at $500,000 and has received $70,000 in cash and a second mortgage on that building for $110,000, totaling $180,000 (his equity), and you have ended up ex-changing a $150,000 building with a $70,000 equity for a $500,000 building with the same $70,000 equity. (I have of course ignored escrow costs and prorations.)

There are two important advantages to you if you exchange as I have just described. The first is that you now own a more valuable building without having paid a nickel in capital-gains taxes to the IRS. The second is that you can now start depre-ciation on this more expensive building. Let's look at some numbers. We first must know the basis of the old building at the time of sale. This is as follows:

Old building:

Original cost of building	$80,000
Less depreciation taken	25,000
Basis	$55,000

What this means is that the building that we traded at valuation of $150,000 was originally bought for $80,000 and that over a period of years, using the old style of depreciation, we had taken a total of $25,000, leaving the basis, or book value, of the building at $55,000.

We now must determine what the gain would have been if we had sold the building rather than exchanged it. This is:

Gain if sold:

Selling price/valuation	$150,000
Less basis	55,000
Gain	$ 95,000

This simply means that if we had sold the building rather than exchanged it, our gain would have been the selling price less the basis, or $95,000.

We need to know this gain if sold because the basis of the new building will be its valuation less the gain if the old building had been sold. Here are the numbers:

New building:

Exchange valuation ("cost")	$500,000
Less "gains" if sold building sold	95,000
Basis of new building	$405,000
Old basis depreciated on old rule	55,000
Balance depreciated by ACRS rules	$350,000

The basis of the new building will be $405,000, which is what it would have cost if you had bought it, less the amount of the gain from the old building rolled-over into the new building, namely $405,000. If the old building had been bought before 1981 and was subject to the old rules, then its prior basis of $55,000 would continue to be depreciated under the old rules. If you had exchanged a newer building and had been taking straight-line depreciation for thirty years for an older building, you could now select 125% declining balance for twenty years if you so chose. However, the remainder of the basis, namely the new basis less that part attributable to the old building, is depreciated by the ACRS rules. In our case this would be the lion's share, or $350,000.

What would the amount of this depreciation be? If we ignore land and assume that the trade was done in January, it would be as follows:

Depreciations

Old building S/L 20 years	$ 4000
New building	
old basis: 55,000 @ S/L 20 years	$ 4000
ACRS basis: 350,000 @ ACRS 15 years	$42,000
Total	$46,000

You can now see the tremendous advantage in exchanging. In addition to not paying any capital-gains tax, the new building will increase depreciation from the old $4000 per year to a new total of $46,000 per year, almost twelve times as much!

It's true that if you had sold and bought, you could have

taken ACRS depreciation on the total purchase price of $500,000 (ignoring land), and that would have been $60,000. It might seem that sale and purchase is better in terms of depreciation, because purchase of a $500,000 building would give a first-year depreciation of $60,000. However, if the prior building is actually sold, then $15,000 to $22,500 must be paid to the government for tax on the gains, and the remaining amount of the equity would not be enough to buy a $500,000 building. So, all in all, it appears that exchanging might be the best alternative.

DELAYED EXCHANGE

We have talked about an exchange where you find your up-property while you are still in escrow to sell the smaller property. But what happens if the eighty-seventh day rolls around and you have not yet found your up-property (the property you want to trade up to) or at least are not in a position to close and the buyer definitely requires that you close on the ninetieth day? You have two choices. You can go ahead and complete the transaction of the sale, pay the capital-gains taxes, and buy a smaller building with your diminished equity. Or you can handle the transaction as a delayed exchange. The IRS says that a delayed exchange does not fulfill the requirements of Section 1031 and wants to disallow it. However, in the most definite court case to date, the Ninth Circuit Court of Appeals (second only to the Supreme Court) has ruled that a deferred exchange is indeed legal. (The taxpayer's name in this case was T. J. Starker, and this kind of exchange is sometimes referred to as a Starker Exchange.)

I have yet to hear of an IRS challenge to a deferred exchange, and if such a thing happens, it will receive immediate and wide dissemination within the income tax fraternity.

What are the mechanics of a delayed exchange? It turns out to be fairly simple. First of all the buyer must agree to cooperate. Since it is clear in the escrow documents that any such cooperation will be at no cost or expense to him, this is never a problem. Given this cooperation, the sale exchange is consummated. At the conclusion of this the buyer owns the property and starts to use it and depreciate it as he or she would any property. In the meantime, however, you, the seller, do not receive the proceeds of the sale. If you did, the exchange would immediately be canceled and it would be treated as a sale. Instead, there is an exchange agreement and a trust agreement such that the proceeds of the purchase transaction are deposited by the buyer in a trust which is independent of both the buyer and the seller. The proceeds are kept in this trust (at interest) until such time as the seller finds his or her up-property, any time from a few weeks to a few months, though it could be for a longer time. When the seller finds his property—say it is the same $500,000 property that we have been talking about (purchasable on the same terms)—he notifies the buyer of the property, who in turn notifies the trust holder to deposit the money in the trust into a purchase escrow for the up-property. The *buyer* then buys the up-property and in the same transaction deeds it to the seller (you), thus completing the exchange, in a delayed fashion.

"BOOT"

If you as exchanger are giving up a larger real estate equity than you are getting, you will want to be compensated for the difference by taking back something extra. For instance, if you are exchanging your $90,000 for a $70,000 equity in the other building, you will want something to compensate you for the missing $20,000. This could be either cash, a note, or a combination of these. In any event, any boot (i.e., any property which is not real estate) that you take back is taxable. This applies to a note as well as cash, but the difference is this: if you take back a note, it is fully taxable—but not until the note is paid off. So if it is an interest-only note for three or five years, you will not have to pay tax until the note is paid off.

REFINANCING

You should know that refinancing is not a taxable event. I know of hardly anybody who has not refinanced at least one or more buildings. In my earlier book, *Financial Genius,* I recommended it as a way to improve your return on equity. I recommended that you finance out, and this was always by means of a refinance. Well, from an income tax standpoint, the good news is that no refinancing is ever taxable at that time. It is not reported to the taxing authorities; the only way it reflects in your income tax return is that the additional interest you pay is deductible. The IRS isn't too worried about the nontaxability; they know they will catch up to you when you sell the building. At that time, the gain will be taxable even though you won't have all the money because you got some of it earlier at the time of refinancing. There is still a way to postpone the tax on refinancing, and that is to exchange.

YOUR LIFETIME PLAN

The combination of the tax-free feature of refinancing and the tax-free feature of exchanging leads to a situation where you may never sell at all. Properly done, after you buy your first property and increase its value, you can refinance it (nontaxable) and use the money to buy other properties and improve them and refinance them (nontaxable). When you want to, you can exchange one or several of them for one or more up-properties, nontaxable. In this way you can increase your net worth, your depreciation, and your appreciation. And, in theory, you can run a hundred-dollar investment into a million-dollar equity. If you die without having sold, none of that million-dollar gain will be taxable at all. This is known as the ultimate loophole! Of course, there are other ways to arrange it involving estate planning. Certainly, when you have a million dollars' worth of gain represented in your portfolio, you probably own more than two million dollars' worth of property, and somewhere along the line you probably would have done some estate planning so your estate could be transferred to your heirs with little or no estate tax.

IS THE TAX BOOGIE MAN GOING TO GET YOU?

The first time I got notification that I was being audited by the IRS, I almost started believing in the boogie man again. That audit scared me to death, even though I really had nothing to hide. An audit is like anything else you experience for the first time: you will be fearful because you don't know what is going to happen. But if you know the facts, you quickly cease to be fearful. The facts are these:

The chances of being audited in the first place are about 2½% overall. Even if you make over $50,000, your chances are still only 8 7/10%. Unless there is fraud, the repercussions of being audited are nominal. Even if you inadvertently left some-thing out of your tax return, which is easy to do, the IRS will no-tify you of such an omission and will ask you to pay the tax owed. No hassle, no big deal. You may have to pay some inter-est, but typically there is no penalty to pay for the omission.

IF YOU'RE NOT GETTING AUDITED OFTEN, YOU'RE PAYING TOO MUCH

If you have a good, honest, aggressive tax man who is helping you with the preparation of your taxes, there is a good chance that you will be audited fairly often. Once you get over the fear, and realize that the IRS is not the boogie man and will not get you, you won't panic when you get a letter from the IRS an-nouncing an audit.

DON'T LET THEM PUT YOU ON THE SPOT

If you walk into an auditor's office and sit there with all your records and he or she asks you a particularly probing, difficult question, you are really on the spot. You are stuck. As you fumble through your papers, you'll start to feel the blood run to your head and you will start to sweat. You have got to come up with an answer right there. And to come up shorthanded makes you look bad. You are convinced that he is thinking, "What else is this guy hiding?" Such an ordeal can easily be avoided by never meeting with the IRS yourself. Have a middle-man do it for you. As discussed in Chapter 8 on negotiating, the middleman method of negotiating can be very effective. It is no different with the IRS. If he asks your tax man a question that he can't or doesn't want to answer on the spot, he can al-ways put the IRS off by saying that he doesn't know the answer to that, that he's going to have to ask his client. That gives your tax man time to think. It gives him time to plan with you in strat-egy meetings. It gives him time to do research on the particular question that comes up. It also gives the IRS agent time to for-get the issue, because like everybody else, the IRS is swamped and backlogged with work.

YOU WON'T GO TO JAIL

If you start to plan now to use a middleman if and when you are audited, it may help you overcome some of the hesitations you have about audits. Some people actually believe that unintentional mistakes they have made on their return could put them in such jeopardy they could go to jail, which is not true. Sure, you can go to jail for absolute out-and-out fraud, but first you have to commit fraud and second they have to prove that you intended to. And that is a long way from where most people are.

YOU DON'T HAVE TO CHEAT

Not long ago I gave a seminar in Santa Barbara, California, in which I talked about tax savings and investing. After the seminar a lady came up to me and confessed that she had not reported over $10,000 interest income for the last few years. She was mad. She was tired of paying taxes and she refused to pay any more. So she wasn't telling the IRS about the interest income.

I told her how dumb that was. I said that she didn't have to do that. With the depreciation laws being so liberal now, it is easy to cut your taxes to zero in totally legitimate ways. Besides, banks, savings and loans, and other financial institutions are required by law to send to the IRS a copy of all the interest paid to all their accounts. The IRS knows if you don't claim interest you have received, so you had better tell them.

Intentionally not reporting income is foolish because you could go to jail for that. But taking maximum deductions of all kinds, even some that are questionable, will not put you in jeopardy. The worst thing that is going to happen if the deduction is disallowed is the IRS will make you pay the taxes that you owe on that deduction. So it's not smart to hide income from the IRS, and it's dumb not to take maximum deductions. The rule of thumb when making deductions is, when in doubt, take it! The worst thing that can happen is they will disallow it and you will pay taxes on it.

Cutting your taxes to zero will speed up the process of your own financial freedom and independence; in fact, it could get you there twice as fast. So it is well worth your time to start taking necessary steps now.

OTHER TAX TOPICS

The subject of income taxes is, of course, a very extensive one and I can't cover it completely in this book. These topics below

and many others are covered in laymen's language in the tax
newsletter *Zeroing in on Taxes*—see the bibliography.

Investment credit for rehabs
The new alternative minimum tax
Installment sale
Dealer or investor?
How to get an extension
How to amend your return
How to handle an audit
How to choose a tax preparer
IRAs & Keoghs
Year-end tax planning

16

THE FEAR FACTOR

Fear is the opposite of courage. It is useful only if it motivates us to overcome fear through direct action. In financial matters, being fearful of risk undermines one's courage to act. With inaction, fears multiply through negative worries and over-imagined dangers. Be brave. Pursue your financial goals with confidence. Remember what Bertrand Russell said: "To conquer fear is the beginning of wisdom." *If you have carefully considered all aspects of a deal and it looks mostly possible, go ahead.* If you have to have a guarantee that everything will be all right before you take a risk, you will never ever get off first base: the future is promised to no one.

ACTION WILL GET YOU MORE THAN $20

Many times in my lectures I take a $20 bill from my wallet and hold it up and say, "Action is really the great separator—it separates the wealthy from the poor, the dissatisfied from the frustrated, even the happy from the unhappy. But most of all, action gets things done, action overcomes fear." Then I ask who would like the $20 bill. Typically, with 300 or 400 people present, only about 100 hands will appear. Sometimes three or four people will use their voices. "I do!" they'll shout. Holding the $20 bill absolutely still and staring straight ahead, I do absolutely nothing. I just stand there like the Statue of Liberty, but with a $20 bill instead of a torch in my hand. I stand there for as long as it takes for someone to take action.

SOMETIMES WE NEED A PUSH

The action that I want is for someone to get up, walk to the front, come up on the stage, and take the $20 bill out of my hand. It is amazing to me how long it takes sometimes. Recently a lady walked up and reached for the bill, but she didn't step up onto the two-foot stage and she couldn't quite reach it. She continued to stand and reach for it as I stood motionless. She looked around at the audience, very embarrassed. She seemed to be caught in the middle. She didn't know what to do. Finally someone in the audience yelled, "Go ahead and take it!" So she stepped up on the stage and finally grabbed it out of my hand, then went back to her seat. Sometimes we need a push from someone else, even from those who aren't brave themselves.

I told the guy in the audience, "Boy, you were really brave to sit there all safe and secure in your seat and yell out to her what she should do. Why didn't you come up and take it yourself?"

Obviously he (and everyone else) was somewhat fearful. It was an embarrassing situation, full of temporary risk, but the lady who got out of her seat and eventually took the money out of my hand admitted her action did help to overcome her fear.

She almost blew it at the last minute by not taking that one last step to get what she was after. And so it is with many people. They get right to the edge of success and they freeze. They choke. They don't know what to do. They don't have quite enough courage to go over the edge, to make that final lunge or step to accomplish their goals.

ACTION GETS THINGS DONE

Besides overcoming fear, action does a lot of other things too. It gets things done; and, after all, that's the whole ball game. Without action you can be the greatest financial thinker, have the highest IQ, and end up broke.

The husband of the lady who came up and got the $20 bill was embarrassed. I asked him what he thought was happening to him. He said, "I don't know, but I didn't want anybody to know that I was with her." She admitted that she felt foolish, too! But as she sat down she won the applause of the entire audience, so who really turned out to be foolish? Her or the 399 people in the audience? Remember the wall plaque in Chapter 1: THE WORLD WILL STAND ASIDE FOR THE PERSON WHO KNOWS WHERE HE IS GOING. Wasn't that demonstrated by the $20-bill incident? The audience stood aside while the woman walked forward and took the $20. Then, after she accomplished her task and sat down, they applauded. They were proud of her. No, they didn't do it themselves, but they were impressed by her courage to do what any one of them could have done.

FEAR OF STARTING

Getting started is really the most frightening and the hardest part of virtually any task. *But even if you do something wrong, at least do something.* I am not saying take risks larger than you can afford. I don't believe in that. I don't think that that is good. One should take risks gradually, whether they are financial risks, social risks, or any other kind of risk. But one does need to *take* risks. To face fear. Then, when you have mastered a small fear, you can go for the bigger ones.

FEAR AND TENSION

Recently, while making the final approach on a flight (I wish they wouldn't call it the *final* approach), I noticed that the lady sitting next to me was very nervous. Thinking that by diverting her attention I could ease her stress, I began talking with her. Then the captain lowered the flaps and the landing gear. She gasped and gripped the arm rests of the seat. Talk about a white-knuckle flyer, this lady was it. I quickly explained to her what had just happened, which gave her only temporary relief because then we hit a little turbulence and bounced up and down. She was obviously very distressed.

I suddenly realized that I was in the same plane, in the same situation, but my heart rate and blood pressure were normal. I patted her hand, but the only thing that came close to helping was each time there was a sudden movement or noise, I explained exactly what was happening, which seemed to calm her a bit. At the end of the flight she was very terribly uptight and not at all rested.

CHRONIC FEAR, NOT FEAR, IS YOUR REAL ENEMY

It was easy to understand how she felt since I had been there too. I knew the damage that fear could do because it had done damage to me in the past. The same thing used to happen to me, but once I realized that I was letting fear dominate my thoughts I decided to do something about it. Since I travel a great deal, and since being relaxed and rested at the end of a flight is important to my performance, it was important not to waste so much energy wrestling with fear.

It didn't take much thinking after that to figure out that the fear factor entered into many of my decisions that had far greater implications than did flying. Why should I let myself be fearful about flying or anything else? After all, does that fear change the outcome of the flight I'm on or my financial conditions? People who are the real doers in life face frightening situations almost every day, but they don't let those confrontations with fear scare them to death or slow down their progress or stop their actions.

PILOT, PRIEST, AND POPE ALL HAVE FEARS

Realizing that everyone has fears is a big first step to overcoming yours. Remember that Buddha's first of the four noble truths is, "Life is suffering." Life is difficult; it really is difficult, not just for you but for everybody. Fully understanding and realizing that can be a major breakthrough in anyone's life. Life is difficult for everyone, rich and poor, fat and skinny, beautiful and ugly, male and female, old and young; and everyone has fears, fears that make life harder. No matter what a person's position is, attorney, CPA, judge, pilot or priest; yes, even an astronaut, the President of the United States, and the Pope have fears. But those people who learn to confront them, try to understand them, and take some action to overcome them, are the people who are truly the successes in this world. They have courage. You see, courage is not existing without fears but it is facing them with actions so you can overcome them.

We have all been in situations where someone has said, "Don't worry, it will be okay. Calm down. There is nothing to worry about." And we all know those words usually don't help.

I totally overcame my fear of flying by understanding the facts and the dynamics of flying. I took action to have understanding. I even took flying lessons. I really confronted my fears. I learned, for example, that it is absolutely impossible for an airplane to fall out of the sky if it's flying faster than stall speed. So no matter how slowly the plane seems to be going, as long as it is flying faster than stall speed, that won't happen.

THE NUMBER-ONE FEAR

Speaking in public is the greatest single fear of Americans. It tops the list way above the fear of dying. I did two things to overcome this fear. First, I gained an understanding of the dynamics of speaking. I learned what makes a good speech. I came to understand both the empathy and the criticism that an audience can and will have. In addition, when I realized that virtually everyone is scared to death of standing in front of an audience and speaking, for some reason that was very, very comforting to me and helped me squarely face my fear.

Second, rather than being frozen in my tracks, I purposely and forcefully pushed myself to apply action to overcome that fear. That is, I began to give speeches and did so many, many times until the fear diminished. In fact, it diminished to the point that I could really be totally myself onstage. And that is when any person really becomes good, for he can then express himself by using his own personality.

SIX COMMON FEARS

Most of us at one time or another in our lives experience many or all of the following fears:

- Fear of making a fool of yourself.
- Fear of winning. Many times you will see people choke up right at the end and go on to lose. This is sometimes an indication of the fear of winning. If you win now, you might always have to perform on the same high level.
- Fear of losing all your money.
- Fear of losing your friends.
- Fear of losing the love and respect of someone you love.
- Fear of criticism.

FIRST-TIME FEARS

I remember back when I bought my first apartment building. It was a run-down twelve-unit building that needed a lot of time and attention. I almost backed out of the closing because of fear.

When we do something for the first time, it's almost always a frightening situation. Why, even going to a restaurant for the first time can be more than a little bit bothersome. You don't know what the menu is or what the prices are (it might be too expensive); you don't know the layout of the restaurant or whether to seat yourself or wait to be seated. All this can produce some anxiety—consequently many people get in the habit of going to the same restaurants, and so, because of trivial fears, won't try new and different places.

Multiply these small anxieties by ten or more, and you have the fear factor I had when buying my first apartment building. Even though it was a super deal with only 6% downpayment, at a very low price, I almost backed out at the last minute. What were my fears? I was afraid of everything: from all the tenants refusing to pay the rent, to all the plumbing going bad the day that I bought it. When you have never bought a building before, your imagination can go wild. Mine did. When you haven't ever bought a $100,000 property before, it scares you to death. The first time I ever bought a $500,000 property, the same thing happened. Ditto with my first million-dollar purchase and again with my first five-million-dollar acquisition!

WHAT TO DO WHEN YOU'RE NOT BRAVE

So what do we do about these fears? Well, first remember that fear is a natural emotion, one that must be understood, confronted, and controlled. In other words, this is an appropriate place to *fake it till you make it.* But you need to do it with action.

WHISTLE A HAPPY TUNE AND NO ONE WILL SUSPECT I'M AFRAID

If we pretend to be brave, acting the way a brave man would act, the results are amazing. Consider the many times you have lain in bed thinking about some tough assignment, something that you are slightly or very fearful of doing. If you've never done it before, quite naturally you are reluctant and anxious. For example, if you are giving a speech for the first time to some important people, or asking a banker for a loan, or presenting an offer to buy a particular property. Or it may be visiting a new state or country, or being a master of ceremonies. In any case, whatever you have to do on that particular day as you lie in bed, if you have a few fears of doing it, they will only intensify the longer you lie there and think about it. What will overcome those frightening thoughts and imaginings is action. *Even if it is incorrect action, get up, get going, and get the blood running.* Take a shower, get on the phone, write letters, go see people, make things happen.

I HAD TO PUT ACTION WHERE MY MOUTH IS

Even though I have a much higher level of confidence now, I find that I still harbor some fears. I was recently in Indianapolis to consult a young, recently divorced mother of three. She didn't have a job and she didn't know how or where to start to get one. She was obviously very much afraid of going out into the marketplace. I was explaining to her how action overcomes fears and how she needed to go out and make things happen. I found myself telling her that she merely needed to get on the phone and start calling people, asking for a job. I said, "All you need to do is pick up the phone and call a business and ask them. It's as simple as that. That's how you overcome fear."

After saying that, I suddenly realized that if it were so easy to do, why didn't I do it and show her how to do it instead of telling her how to do it? So I asked what kind of business she would like to work for. She said she had always wanted to work in a floral shop. I grabbed the phonebook, turned to "florists" in the Yellow Pages, and dialed the first number I saw. As soon as the phone rang I could feel my heart rate increase and I was actually nervous, very nervous in fact. I was surprised at my nervousness and the fear I was experiencing. As the phone rang, my "self-talk" went something like this: "I can't believe that I am afraid of making a phone call to some dumb little floral shop. But heavens, I can't stop now, she's watching and I'm trying to prove something to her. I am onstage."

About that time, a young man answered and asked if he could help me. I began by saying, "I understand that you have been looking for some extra help in your shop, and I have a friend who would be excellent for the position." The young man hesitated a bit and said, "Well, I'm not sure that we do. Well, I guess. Well, I don't really know . . . let me have you talk to the manager." In a few moments the manager was on the line. I said the same thing to him and to my amazement he said that he hadn't really been looking for anybody, but he could use an extra person. So I proceeded to describe the young mother to him and actually set up an appointment then and there for her to come and meet him and apply for a job. I wrote down the time and his name and hung up.

I then turned to her and said, keeping a straight face the whole time, "See how easy it is—you just have to do it." Later, I did tell her that I had had some fearful thoughts as I dialed and as I spoke to the shop owner, but that action helped me overcome being scared as I got into the conversation with him. I could easily have made the next phone call since I was successful on the first one and feeling quite sure of myself by then. What I was doing was faking it until I made it. I was acting as if I had courage when actually I had some less-than-brave thoughts.

FEARS ARE MENTAL

Action overcomes fear because most fears are in your mind and action lets the physical part of you dominate for a while. The physical side of you needs to dominate because the mental side, in cases like this, becomes too introspective and too analytical. We tend to analyze to death. We have all heard of "analysis paralysis," which is more than two cute rhyming words.

Sometimes we think too much. In today's educated, deep-thinking, and analyzing world, we have a lot more planners and thinkers and analyzers than we do action people. Obviously we do need some kind of plan, but the greatest plan in the world is worthless without action. I would much rather have a mediocre plan and some real action people to carry it out than the most phenomenal plan in the world and a bunch of inactive people.

I HAVE A CAREER TO BUILD

On a flight to Dallas, Texas, I eavesdropped on a conversation between two musicians sitting in front of me. One was telling the other how anxious he was to have more of his music published. He had gone to a publisher who told him there would be an eighteen-month delay but they would nevertheless publish his music. He told the publisher that he couldn't wait that long, and he wouldn't, so he turned them down flat, saying, "I have a career to build." What a great line. It was like he was building the World Trade Towers and he had a deadline he had to meet.

If all of us looked at our own projects, financial and otherwise, with this same attitude and intensity; if we looked at each thing we did as a stepping-stone or building block in our own career and thought that we had to build it within twelve months (or twenty-four or forty-eight), we would be so much better off. Most deadlines, however, are set by others, and if we don't have the deadline we don't get the work done.

MAKE YOUR DEADLINE A DEAD LINE

Originally a deadline was a line drawn within or around a prison that meant just what it sounds like: cross the line and they shot you dead. Failing to set and to meet financial deadlines can kill us off, too, in the business world. Knowing this, we should force our own selves to overcome fear by taking the action to do so. In other words, in a way, we can use fear to overcome fear—the fear of being shot down versus the fear of acting in some way or doing something we really want to do. It's a mental game in a way. Down that mental road we go, reminding ourselves that the deadline is very important, even critical, and the consequences of missing it are more to be feared than the actions needed to meet it. Be courageous—do it!

When we finally let go of fear, we see and act at levels beyond what we have imagined possible. It is then and only then that we begin to discover our real selves and take advantage of our full potential.

EGO MUSCLE

To go to the top financially you have to have a fair-sized ego, but that ego can't be so large that it gets in your way. When you recognize you have weaknesses, you certainly don't want your ego to foolishly stop you from borrowing someone else's talents, talents that can shore up your weakness.

I have never met a person in my life who has total confi-

dence in himself or herself. There is not one of us who won't have some serious questions about our own ability to succeed as we start a new venture.

We can gain great courage by looking at others and seeing what they have done. As we realize we can do it too, we start to grow.

A NATURAL BENT WORTH $120,000 TO THIS LOVELY LADY

A divorced woman by the name of Edna uprooted herself and her small son from a quiet town in Visalia, California, and moved to Santa Barbara. After a year there, during which her savings were depleted almost to zero, she bought a small corner grocery store that was struggling and ready to go under.

But she had some ideas. She had some plans and dreams. You see, she believed in herself. And fortunately she had a few people around that also believed in her and bolstered her up when her confidence lagged a little bit. Did she have experience in owning and running a grocery store? No, none whatsoever. But she took the time to learn a little bit about the business. In fact, she threw herself totally into it, spending countless hours reading and researching, studying the neighborhood, and trying to isolate what the problem was with the little corner store. After she felt that she had most of the answers, she took the dive; she plunged into it, putting in over $25,000, which was virtually every penny she had. It was a do or die, sink or swim, situation.

Was she scared? You bet she was scared. Her fear pushed her to work far beyond anything anyone expected of her except herself. She did it. She was successful. A year later she could have sold the store and walked away with a handsome $120,000 profit. Not bad for a twenty-seven-year-old who was burdened with many other responsibilities.

Edna followed her natural bent. She loved people and wasn't afraid of long hours. She knew she had to pay attention to the right details or her profit margins would vanish. She had the courage to succeed, the courage to be rich. So can you.

AFTERWORD

The techniques, formulas, and methods that I've covered in this book are all necessary and very important, but without the courage to take action you can know everything there is to know and die penniless. Remember: Courage, or Guts, is not for hire. Only you can supply it, and to supply it you have to develop it. And that process takes place between your ears, usually when you are all alone having a talk with yourself, being your own coach. Just about anyone can read a book or hear a speech and get all excited and motivated about what he or she is going to accomplish, but the only thing that really counts in a race is who crosses the finish line. Beginning is sometimes easy; to go all the way is tough. Just knowing and expecting to get discouraged or to experience minor setbacks should help you when you hit those barriers. When you find yourself there, go back and recharge your mental or courage battery by rereading this book or attending a seminar. Remember: courage is going against the odds and holding up in the face of criticism. It's not giving up when you are discouraged or have setbacks. You can lose a player or two in the orchestra, but the leader is indispensable.

Everyone in your financial orchestra needs to be told what to do. You, as their leader, need to dig deep within yourself to know what to tell them to do, because no one is there to help you. I believe that our Creator built us with all the equipment we need to know what to do with, but much of it is hidden down deep somewhere in the gray matter of our minds. And without some hard work and introspection, you'll never find it. You'll never rise to the top. But with mental effort and toughness, you will find it and get out in front and lead. The personal and financial rewards will be so great and satisfying that you will look back at the person you used to be and hardly recognize that self.

It's your life, not anyone else's, so why not take advantage of the time allotted to you and really go for it. A person who lets himself go completely, unfettered, totally throwing himself into whatever he is doing (whether it is playing a sport, giving a speech, or reading a book) can ignore distracting obstacles, setbacks, and discouragements and reach phenomenal heights of success. When it's all over, he will say he was playing (or participating) "out of my mind." You see, these men and women have reached a higher consciousness, but that state is closer to their true selves. So go ahead, have courage, let go a little and unleash your true self and see what you can accomplish with the balance of time remaining in your life. After all, you're going to die someday so why not really live instead of just existing? Really go for it and see what you can become. I think you'll be surprised. I was!

BIBLIOGRAPHY

Blackwell, Dale. *How to Think Your Way to Financial Independence.* Salt Lake City, Utah: National Institute of Financial
Planning, 1978. 1831 Ft. Union Blvd., Dept. PN, Salt Lake
City, UT. 84121. This book is a must to help you develop
your ability to think clearly.

Campbell, David. *Take the Road to Creativity and Get Off Your
Dead End.* Niles, Illinois: Argus Communications, 1977. I
read this book in about two hours and generated a lot of
ideas on creativity.

Dyer, Wayne. *Pulling Your Own Strings.* New York: Thomas Y.
Crowell, 1978. Dyer gives sound advice on how to become your own person, which is essential if you want to
build your courage factor.

Financial Freedom Report. Salt Lake City, Utah: The National
Institute of Financial Freedom. 1831 Ft. Union Blvd., Dept.
PN, Salt Lake City, UT. 84121. A monthly financial magazine for investors or potential investors in income-producing properties. It tells how to find, negotiate, finance, and
buy properties. It also covers income taxes for the begin-
ners.

Haroldsen, Mark O. *Goals, Guts and Greatness.* Salt Lake
City, Utah: The National Institute of Financial Freedom,
1978. 1831 Ft. Union Blvd., Dept. PN, Salt Lake City, UT.
84121. This is my second book. It deals mainly with self-
motivation and the principles of success used by several
highly successful people. I think it is a terrific book, but of
course I am somewhat biased.

————. *How to Master Your Financial Destiny.* Salt Lake City,

Utah: The National Institute of Financial Planning, 1979. 1831 Ft. Union Blvd., Dept. PN, Salt Lake City, UT. 84121. This book contains numerous standard forms with accompanying explanations that are very helpful in presenting offers and properties, analyzing them and buying them. Plus financial forms for bank loans and many others.

————. *How to Wake Up the Financial Genius Inside You.* Salt Lake City, Utah: The National Institute of Financial Freedom, 1982. 1831 Ft. Union Blvd., Dept. PN, Salt Lake City, UT. 84121. This book tells my story from the first step forward: how I got started, how I bought my first few properties with little or no cash. If you are just starting and want to buy real property, this book will save you time and mistakes. Book can be ordered by telephone: 801-943-1280.

Kroc, Ray. *Grinding It Out.* Chicago: Berkley Publications, 1977. The man who made McDonald's Hamburgers what it is today tells his own story. From a salesman of milkshake mixers, find out how Ray Kroc became the hamburger king.

Lee, Dick. *How to Pay Zero Income Tax—Legally.* Pacific Palisades, CA: Lambda Publishing, 1982. If you paid zero tax on your Federal returns for 1980, 1981, or 1982, mail a photocopy of each qualifying Federal return. Send photocopies only; nothing will be returned. Send only your Federal returns, no state returns. If you qualify, Dick will contact you further to arrange for amending returns and claiming the refund. Send your returns to: Lee Tax Service, 1085 Ravoli Drive, Pacific Palisades, CA 90272.

Maltz, Maxwell. *Psycho Cybernetics.* New York: Simon and Schuster, 1960. An old classic but still worth reading.

Neill, Humphrey B. *The Art of Contrary Thinking.* Caldwell, Idaho: Caxton Publishers, 1963. Develop a new way of looking at situations, arguments, or ideas. This book will stretch your mind to consider the other side of the idea.

Peck, Scott. *The Road Less Traveled.* New York: Simon and Schuster, 1979. Probably the best book I have ever read that deals with coping with life, what love is and what it isn't, the difference between falling in love and real loving, dependency and independency. You'll love this one!

Peters, Thomas J., and Robert H. Waterman. *In Search of Excellence.* New York: Harper and Row, 1982. Studying a group of Fortune 500 companies, Peters and Waterman have drawn conclusions about what has made these companies successful. Some of the findings are not what we would traditionally expect. This is the real world of business today and what it takes to make a successful company.

Sill, Sterling W. *How to Personally Profit From the Laws of Success.* Salt Lake City, Utah: The National Institute of Financial Planning, 1981. 1831 Ft. Union Blvd., Dept. PN, Salt Lake City, UT. 84121. The best nonfinancial motivation book I have ever read. Sterling Sill has written over thirty books. At age eighty, he is still going strong.

Zeroing In on Taxes. Salt Lake City, Utah: The National Institute of Financial Planning. 1831 Ft. Union Blvd., Dept. PN, Salt Lake City, UT. 84121. An excellent monthly tax newsletter that keeps you updated on what you can do to zero-out your taxes every year.

A Challenge From
Mark O. Haroldsen
To The Readers of This Book:

Who Are You Really? I try to picture what you look like. That's right. As I write this book I try to picture the faces of the people who will be reading each page. Are you young or old, male or female? It is an interesting exercise, but admittedly, I don't know much about you.

But I do know that somewhere inside you is a dream. A dream to be wealthy. Otherwise you would never have purchased this book.

The World Is Full of Dreamers. You can go downtown and look on any street you choose and you'll find dreamers. People who dream of having more, of doing more, of having a better life. But most people will never do more than dream. Of the thousands of people who buy this book about 75 percent will read it. And studies tell me that only 40 percent will consider putting into effect these principles and techniques.

Are You One of the 20%? But only 20% will actually go out and give it a try. That amazes me. All the dreamers in the world, but only 20% that will actually DO SOMETHING! That's why the median income in the U.S. today is only about $15,000 a year. People are content to remain "average" even when presented with an opportunity to become a "superstar."

Do Something Now. As I mentioned in Chapter I it isn't that hard to become financially free. All it takes is information and action. I'm making the information, knowledge, and techniques available, but the action part is up to you. You've read the book, now either put it down and continue dreaming like 80% of the population or get going now.

Here's some extra help. For those who are really serious about getting going the book is usually not enough. They want more. More valuable information. That's why the Financial Freedom Report exists. It is a confidential monthly report just for people like you on their way to financial freedom. It isn't available on any newstand. It contains step-by-step instruction on a monthly basis. Sure you can become wealthy without the Financial Freedom Report, it just takes longer.

Study 12 reports risk-free. The report sells for $38 per year. People who have taken it for years think that the price is ridiculously low (but most of them are wealthy now). But I'll make you a special offer. I'll send you 12 sealed issues of the Financial Freedom Report right now for only $14.95. But that's not all. I'll give you 3 months to read them and give the information a real test. See if it works. If it does you've made a wise investment (about the price of three movie tickets). If you don't do anything in three months send the reports back and I'll refund your money plus $2 for your efforts. That's right, I'll send you back **$16.95** if you aren't completely satisfied.

Get started now. If you've got a credit card pick up the phone and dial 1-801-943-1280 and tell them you want the special sealed report package. Or send your check for $14.95 to Sealed Reports, Dept. PN, 1831 Fort Union Blvd., Salt Lake City, Utah 84121. Remember, it's guaranteed.

Cash from Banks. For a free report on how to borrow from $20,000 to $200,000 on your signature write "How to Borrow" to the above address.